JEANCHRÉTIEN
a Legacy of
SCANDAL

BY PAUL TUNS

FREEDOM PRESS (CANADA) INC.
JORDAN, ONTARIO

JEAN CHRETIEN:
A Legacy of Scandal

Layout and cover design: Jason Bouwman

Published by Freedom Press (Canada) Inc.
Jordan, Ontario, Canada

First Edition

ISBN 0-9732757-2-3

Printed in the United States of America

For
Patrick, Michael and Kathryn

CONTENTS

ACKNOWLEDGEMENTS

No book is solely the work of one person and *Jean Chretien: A Legacy of Scandal* is no exception. But to break with tradition, I want to thank my wife Christina first. Without her assistance, sacrifice, support, encouragement and understanding, this book would not have been possible. Originally this book was to be ready for the Spring 2004 election, but because the publishing industry is as unpredictable as a government's election call, it was not to be. Still, the original draft was written in less than a month, mostly in the evenings after a full day at work. If Christina didn't say "Don't worry about the house or kids for one month, I'll take care of everything," I would not have been able to write what you have in your hands right now. I can never repay her for shouldering both our responsibilities at home for four weeks. But she went beyond the call of wifely devotion when she read the first draft and assisted with the research, including reading one book and the tedious task of finding specific articles. I also thank my children, Patrick, Michael and Kathryn for their patience and sacrifice as their dad neglected too many of his fatherly duties while he completed his authorly duties. I hope we never have to endure that again.

Early copies of the manuscript were looked at, commented upon and improved by Adam Daifallah, Gerry Nicholls and Stephen Tardif. Adam is a *National Post* editorial writer and co-author (with Peter G. White) of one of the most important source books for this volume, *Gritlock: Are the Liberals in Forever?* Gerry is vice president of the National Citizen's Coalition. Stephen is a friend of mine who is studying philosophy and literature at the University of Toronto. To each of them, thank you for your meticulous reading and constructive critiques of the manuscript. From deleting extraneous passages to developing or elaborating on certain points or noting subtleties I failed to appreciate, their suggestions improved the flow of the narrative and force of the arguments. I'm deeply indebted to all three for their time and consideration and critical eye. Of course, they bear no responsibility for the final product.

I would also like to thank Ezra Levant for generously agreeing to write the foreword. A better summary of why this book was necessary could not be made.

I want to thank everyone at Freedom Press (Canada) Inc., especially my copy editors, Joanne Byfield and Al Siebring. Their suggestions and corrections made this a better, more readable book. And to Jason Bouwman for designing the cover; even if I had artistic talent, I'd be envious of the work he does.

Paul Tuns - *Toronto, July 2004*

FOREWORD

It is difficult for many Canadians to name any great legacy left by Jean Chretien, despite his ten-year reign as prime minister. As Paul Tuns meticulously documents, though, it isn't hard to name a dozen small legacies – all of which can properly be called scandals.

In Chretien, Canada had a grifter as a prime minister – a small-time finagler who wasn't motivated by grand schemes or ideology, as was Pierre Trudeau and perhaps Brian Mulroney. No Charter of Rights or Canada-U.S. Free Trade Agreement for him; it wasn't about new ideas, it was about maintaining things just the way they were.

To Chretien, the Canadian principle of peace, order and good government simply meant a government with Chretien at the helm. As Tuns outlines, sometimes that meant Chretien tacked to the right – or at least allowed his government to slowly drift that way with the economic tide of the 1990s. But mainly "good government" meant simply never admitting to doing anything bad – from ministerial scandals to the politically-motivated RCMP Airbus vendetta against Mulroney. The lengths to which Chretien would go to save face – to cover up, and then to cover up the cover-ups – suggest that perhaps Nixon, and not Trudeau, was his political model.

But while Chretien's term as prime minister will likely be regarded by historians as one of Canada's least important, it is important that it be understood. Not just an accurate historical record is at stake – and there, Tuns' research is exemplary, documenting every scandal and foul up of note. But it is important, too, because under Chretien Canada's slide to mediocrity increased in pace. Here is where Tuns shines – drawing together the dozens of little embarrassments, excesses and fiascos into a theme, that the Chretien years were years of slow degeneration, like a bone gradually deprived of calcium. Tuns' catalogue of problems, from the wasteful firearms registry to the systematic destruction of the independence of individual MPs, tells us just how far Canada has slipped from Laurier's dream of a Canadian century.

It is important that the story of Chretien be told, and be told by a serious researcher and a passionate critic like Tuns, for one of the hangovers of Chretienism is a monotonously liberal media/cultural class, the very people who would rechristen Chretien's slouching failure as a proud victory. Tuns' documentary, the first of note since Chretien's retirement, will be an important starting point for any other histories on the era. And it will also form a useful backdrop against which to judge Paul Martin, Chretien's impatient successor, inheritor of Chretien's problems – including various policy time-bombs, like the Kyoto Protocol – and in fact the author of some of Chretien's policies himself. In this book, Tuns demonstrates again why he's become one of Canada's most influential commentators. With his strong research, his unvarnished recitation of the facts, and his cool headed but cutting analysis, he sets the bar for judging Canada's political juggernaut of the 1990s.

Ezra Levant – *Publisher, Western Standard*

CHAPTER 1

PRIME MINISTER BY DEFAULT

The Liberal Party under Prime Minister Jean Chretien dominated politics in the 1990s and early 2000s, winning three consecutive majority governments. It was the first party to achieve this feat since World War II, and Chretien was the first party leader to do it since Mackenzie King. The Liberals banished the other parties to the political wilderness, and even those that attained Official Opposition status were held to fewer than 75 seats. The Tories, the party that was replaced in the 1993 election, were humiliated with just two seats in Parliament when the votes were all counted at the end of that election night. Why did this happen? Up to this point, only a wartime government had enjoyed such success. Indeed, fighting the forces of fascism understandably unites a nation and leads to the kind of victories that Prime Minister King enjoyed. But why did Jean Chretien enjoy similar success?

Part of the reason certainly has to do with historical context. In the 1993 election, it became clear that the country wanted to close the book on Brian Mulroney and his chapter of Canadian history. In doing so, they were forced almost by default, to turn to the Liberals. And indeed, Chrétien was not voted in; Mulroney was voted out. As historian Michael Bliss said of Chretien in *Right Honourable Men*, "In 1993 [he] got to become prime minister because [he was] the leader of the Liberal Party and there was no alternative." Chretien's opponents, wrote Bliss, "were in their worst disarray in their history."[1]

The election became a referendum on the Mulroney years, and Canadians seemed determined to vote for anyone but the Tories. The basic electoral reality was that Liberals were the non-Tories in more ridings in the country than any other party. To be sure, the Bloc Quebecois were the non-Tories in Quebec, winning 54 of 75 seats. And the emerging Reform Party took the bulk of the non-Tory vote in BC and Alberta, winning 46 of 58 seats available in those two provinces. Contrary to the perception that the West voted overwhelmingly in favour of the upstart Reformers though, a close look at the numbers shows that the rest of the West, (Saskatchewan and Manitoba), were not terribly kind to Preston Manning's party, giving him only five of the 26 seats available. But the balance in those two provinces was fairly evenly divided between the Liberals and the NDP, again proving the point that Canadians *were* voting for anyone but the Tories in this election. And the Liberals were clearly the non-Tories of choice in Canada's most populous province, Ontario, and in Atlantic Canada, where they won all but one seat. Indeed, they picked up enough seats in the remaining provinces to form a substantial majority. When the Tories self-destructed and a more conservative Reform Party emerged, Canada was perfectly situated for a Liberal renaissance.

Many commentators who seem favourably disposed toward the Liberal Party of Canada have made reference to the notion that somehow the Liberals are Canada's "Natural Governing Party". It sounds conceited, and undoubtedly it is, but looking at the political history of the last century, and particularly the history of the final decade of that century, the observation seems to be borne out.

After 1993, the Chretien Liberals went on to win the next two elections by being less scary than their opponents. The political reality of 1993 – reinforced in the minds of the Chretien Liberals in two subsequent elections – was that their party was the Natural Governing Party largely by default, because voters truly felt they had no other place to go. The Liberals' political opponents were not governments in waiting: separatists had formed the Official Opposition by winning the majority of seats in Quebec, while the Reform and Progressive Conservatives were desperately working to remain separate from one another, with the former besmirched as small-minded, parochial extremists and the latter dismissed as the leftover rump of a tired and corrupt government. In the midst of all this, the NDP was occupying a narrow ideological strip on the left side of the political spectrum.

Such political realities were an undeniable part of the electoral success for Jean Chretien and his Liberals, and led to what might even have been an understandable degree of arrogance. But under Chretien's leadership, that arrogance led to repeated scandals, poor government and the constriction of democracy. If you recall the decade in which Jean Chretien held power, what comes to mind? You would be hard-pressed to name any significant new policy initiatives or grand visions that animated the government's actions. Pierre Trudeau had his Constitutional Repatriation, his Charter of Rights, and his "Just Society". What did ten consecutive years of Jean Chretien governance produce? What new entitlement or foreign policy initiative? There is no lasting mark of which the government could be proud.[i] There was

---

i. I want to be clear that I don't think sweeping new policy initiatives are necessarily good as an end in themselves, even though that idea certainly animates the mind of the typical Liberal, at least in Ottawa.

only a string of broken promises and a series of scandals – Canada still has the GST and free trade and no (truly) independent ethics counselor. On Jean Chretien's watch, the country also endured the botched Somalia investigation, the Airbus affair, the APEC scandal, the HRDC boondoggle, Shawinigate and, as we discovered after Chretien left office, Adscam. The laundry list of scandals and other improprieties is much longer, more serious, and certainly no less expensive to the Canadian taxpayer than anything that came out of the Mulroney years.

Yet, despite what was either incorrigible corruption or demonstrable incompetence, Canadian voters re-elected the Liberal government twice. Why?

The simple answer is that Canada has slowly become something of a one-party state. And the reasons for this are more complex than the disunity that rules the political Right with the Reform/Canadian Alliance and Progressive Conservative parties butting heads with one another instead of with their common enemies in the Liberal Party. While it's true that the Right was not united, the Liberal Party also absorbed more of the Left, leaving the NDP fighting for official party status. Even if the Right had been united in the 1990s as it is today, it would still have fought an uphill battle against a Liberal Party that faced no significant challenge on its left flank from the NDP.

As it became increasingly clear that the Liberal hegemony would go unchallenged, two things happened. The government became less worried about defending some of its more misguided actions such as an ineffective and expensive gun registry and its support of same-sex "marriage". And simultaneously, the government became much more bold in its defense of its ethical lapses. Very few of Jean Chretien's cabinet ministers were forced to resign and those that did often returned to the cabinet table very quickly.

Chretien came to power on the heels of a severely tarnished Mulroney government, one purportedly as corrupt as Richard Nixon's White House of the early 1970s. Chretien tapped into that feeling, saying, "Canadians feel alienated from their political institutions and they want to restore integrity to them. ... They have had enough of the abuses of Parliament and the arrogance of government."[2] During the election campaign in October of 1993, he promised to lead a much more ethical government. And he promised to lead by example.

He came into office fashioning himself and his government as the antidote to the Mulroney-style corruption he was replacing. Yet he left office setting the standard for unethical or otherwise unacceptable behaviour so low that no one in government was culpable for anything. Chretien dealt with ethics problems in his government by denying there were ethics problems. He would often claim, both for himself and others, that they were only doing their duties as MPs.

The root problem for the Liberals and the country was the overwhelming victories scored by the Liberals in 1993 and in subsequent elections. The Liberals began to believe their own press – that they *were* the "Natural Governing Party." As David Frum has often noted, the Liberals have governed Canada for "80 of the past 108 years, a record unequalled either by the Mexico Party of the Institutional Revolutionary or by the Communist Party of the Soviet Union." Frum continues: "The federal Liberals are not just the most successful political organization in the democratic world – they are the most successful political organization in the world, democratic or not."[3] The Chretien Liberals interpreted the historical fact of the party's electoral dominance, especially the period from 1993-2003, as proof of its almost divinely-ordained dominance in Canadian politics. In fact, rather than reminding themselves that their power came from electoral wins which were nothing more than, in some sense, accidents of history, they started to consider their position of power as a political birthright. At the Conservative Party leadership convention in March of 2004 Alberta Premier Ralph Klein, the convention's keynote speaker, castigated the Liberals for acting like they own Canada. "They actually think they own the country," he said. "Canada is not a commodity. You cannot have a title to the country."

But Chretien's Liberal Party had come to see the public trust it held not as a mandate, but as an entitlement.

This created a very dangerous mind-set among the ruling class of the Liberal Party. If forming the government was a Liberal right, then the party and its top leadership could do no wrong. In fact, the notion that the party had a right to govern would then justify practically any ethical lapses. Ruthless and unwarranted attacks on opponents, unaccounted spending of millions of dollars for the "greater good" of national unity (Adscam), and the invocation of closure on debate over controversial issues such as gay "marriage" and hate crimes legislation could all be justified. In fact, in some instances, the party insiders and Cabinet ministers began equating Liberal policy with the very virtues of "being Canadian." For example, former Justice Minister Martin Cauchon declared gay "marriage" to be a "Canadian value."[4]   The Liberals felt they could do absolutely anything to push through their agenda. After all, the public would forgive them. The public *would just have to* forgive them because they were, after all, the "Natural Governing Party."

It was this kind of thinking that led to the unparalleled arrogance of the Chretien years. The litany of scandals were not an aberration, they were the norm. They were not a symptom of Chretien's arrogance, but the natural conclusion and outworking of that arrogance.

Indeed, the most serious scandal to mark the Chretien years is not found in any particular misdeed, but rather in Chretien's arrogance itself; his blasé dismissal of every criticism. In many ways, his attitude was far worse than his actual behaviour. Chretien's view of his own power as beyond question was a threat to the very ideal of democracy, and a danger to the country he governed.

Indeed, Chretien's attitude is worse because any government that does not serve with a recognition that it is in power at the pleasure of the people quickly becomes corrupt. Once a government loses the notion that it can be defeated at the polls, it begins to act differently. It does things – paying off friends, excusing corruption, recycling old ideas, ramming through legislation without the input of backbench MPs or the opposition – merely because it can. The fact that a government *can* get away with shutting down an independent inquiry, interfering with the actions of the RCMP, or breaking its promises with immunity and impunity leads to a much greater likelihood that a government *will* do these things. And do them over and over again.

In this way, the Chretien Liberals knew they could get away with whatever shenanigans they tried. Canadian voters, especially those in Ontario, would either forgive them, give them the benefit of the doubt, tolerate their misdeeds, or simply not vote. For many of those voters, there was no one else to vote for. And since most of the Ontario voters did not view the Opposition as a serious alternative, the Chretien Liberals benefited. For more than a decade, Jean Chretien ruled Canada. Yet, near the end of his tenure, he scrambled to find a legacy (his patronage appointments were presumably taken care of). It is a telling commentary that any prime minister has so little to show for himself after 10 years in power.

Instead of governing, the Chretien Liberals were consumed by politics. Most of the real policy debates in the 1990s were not between the government and the opposition parties but between Jean Chretien and his Finance Minister, Paul Martin. And unfortunately, many of those debates were not about what policy would best serve Canada. Rather they served as sparring matches in the unending battle between these two men to hold/gain the leadership of the party and thus the country.

Furthermore, elections were not called when a new mandate was needed, but rather when they best served the interests of the Liberal party. This would be less galling if Chretien actually had a goal, a vision, or some thing useful he wanted to do with the power he was seeking. But for Chretien, the battle cry of four more years was an end in itself. It became a matter of power for its own sake. Indeed, Chretien and his government seemed more interested in holding onto power so they could reward their friends. A *Toronto Star* headline about Adscam put it succinctly: "Your money, their friends."[5]

When looking for a legacy, Chretien could easily have found one. But it would hardly be something for which would want to be remembered: scandal, patronage, petty politics and the centralization of power in the Prime Minister's Office dominated his years in power. The only real success that can be clearly identified out of the Chretien years is political. The decade from the early '90's until 2004 was an almost unprecedented success for the Liberal Party. But that success gave the Party such a dose of arrogance that it thought it could get away with anything. And for a decade, it did.

CHAPTER 2

BEING AND NOTHINGNESS

---

peter C. Newman once commented that Jean Chretien's first term (1993-1997) was undistinguished, notable only for two accomplishments: scrapping the replacement purchase for the military's aging Sea King helicopters and scuttling the privatization of the Toronto airport. Whether those two initiatives were all that distinguished that period is debatable, but it is worth noting that these were the two main promises from the 1993 campaign that Chretien did keep in his first term in office.

In 1993, Chretien vowed to scrap a deal for new helicopters that had recently been inked by the Mulroney government. That deal authorized the purchase of 43 EH-101 Cormorant helicopters to replace 32 outdated, 32-year-old Sea King and 15 Labrador helicopters. Noting the Cold War was over, Chretien said there was no reason for the "Cadillac" version of the 'copters. The Liberals seemed to support nixing the deal for no other reason than that it had originally been signed by the Tories. Later, Chretien would use the "savings" from not purchasing the

Cormorant helicopters for a job creation program, ignoring the nearly half-billion dollar cost of not respecting the signed contract and the policy implications of neglecting the material needs of the Armed Forces. Historian J.L. Granatstein says the Liberal attitude towards the military led to the slow neglect of the Canadian forces, and that this neglect was clearly foreshadowed by the cancellation of the helicopter deal.[6] By the end of the Chretien era, the helicopters still had not all been replaced. The government did buy a handful of small search and rescue helicopters – only 15 of them – which were finally pressed into service in 2003. In his pride, Chretien refused to admit a mistake had been made on this file. In fact, he wouldn't even consider bids from the company whose deal the government originally nixed in spite of the government's 1994 White Paper that admitted, "there is an urgent need for robust and capable new ship borne helicopters." The report said that the procurement process for the Sea King replacements has been "hampered at every turn by political meddling."[7] In 2004, the military continues to use the now 40-year-old Sea Kings, "jeopardizing both their missions and their crew."[8] It is a tragedy that the lives of Canada's service personnel are put at risk because of Chretien's vanity.

And it was vanity, even more than the low priority National Defence was given by the government, that left Canada without proper and safe helicopters to the very end of Chretien's mandate. In his book *Right Honourable Men*, Michael Bliss contrasted the issue of the helicopter contract and the general downturn in military spending to the extravagantly expensive gun registry that was being pushed through over every reasoned objection. The Chretien Liberals, wrote Bliss, had "a soft spot for counting guns rather than buying or shooting them."[9]

Bliss, a University of Toronto historian, said Chretien's neglect of the military – he called the Canadian Forces the "'*Antiques Road Show*' of military technology" – threatened its ability to take part in the one activity of which Canadians were genuinely proud: peacekeeping.

Chretien, he said, enjoyed committing Canadian forces to peacekeeping missions but could not because "his government found it so hard actually to deliver that eventually his helpful musings were ignored" by the UN and our allies.[10] In Kosovo in 1999 and Afghanistan in 2001-2002, Bliss noted, Canada could not live up to its military commitments.

It quickly became clear that the government was adrift, all sail and no anchor. Traditionally the Liberal Party has offered grand visions, or at least grand (and expensive) programs, that sought to put the particular administration's mark on the Canadian landscape. But the goal of Chretien's governance seemed less focused on implementing particular policies than it did on holding office as an end in itself.

Granted, sometimes all that is needed is a caretaker government, simple administrators who ensure the smooth running of the ship of state. This seemed to be the vision of Chretien's role for himself and his government.

Not that there wasn't an agenda for the Liberal Party: During the 1993 campaign, Jean Chretien trotted out the Red Book, the 112-page sleek list of promises the Liberals would deliver in the next four years. *Globe and Mail* columnist Jeffrey Simpson recalls that Chretien "carried his Red Book, like a preacher carrying a Bible, and replied whenever questioned about his intentions, 'They're in the Red Book'."[11] Chretien even went so far as to say that the utility of the document was that voters could use it as a checklist to keep tabs on how well the Liberal government kept its commitments to the Canadian public: "You can come with this book in front of me every week after I'm the Prime Minister and say, 'Where are you with your promises, Mr. Chretien?' And we are going to check – I'm telling you everything that is written there I intend to implement."

The gimmick, released on September 17, was successful, in part because election-time manifestos were uncommon (this was in the age just before the Common Sense Revolution in Ontario and Newt Gingrich's "Contract With America" in the 1994 U.S. Congressional elections). The Liberal campaign took off after that, pulling ahead of the Tories to the point that it was not even close. Liberal pollster Michael Marzolini said the document was important as a signal to voters that the party could be held accountable, as it was for the content that it promised.[12]

A centrepiece of the Red Book, indeed, of the entire Liberal campaign in 1993, was the elimination of the GST. By the 1996 budget, Finance Minister Paul Martin's third, the dreaded Goods and Services Tax was still in place. But Martin delivered the bad news to Chretien that with the government beginning to tackle the deficit through significant cuts to transfer payments and changes to the system of unemployment insurance, it was not possible to scrap the GST *and* stay on track to a balanced budget. The GST was a cash cow that the government could not do without. The '96 budget came and the GST remained.

Chretien defended not scrapping the hated tax, maintaining he never promised to eliminate the GST, that technically the Red Book had only said a Liberal government would replace it. Chretien's own ambivalence went back to 1989 when the Tories proposed the GST. During the Liberal leadership race, Chretien would not commit to abolishing or keeping the GST, saying it was irresponsible to promise to do something about it without telling the public what the Liberals intended to put in its place to raise revenues. However, the Red Book directed the Finance Committee of the House of Commons to, within its first year, "report on all options for alternatives to the current GST." It added: "A Liberal government will replace the GST with a system that generates equivalent revenues, is fairer to consumers and to small business, minimizes disruption to small business, and promotes federal-provincial co-operation and harmonization."[13] Indeed, the Finance Department examined alternatives but all were found deficient compared to the existing GST.

After it became clear to the public that the Liberal government was not going to address eliminating the GST, Chretien said the party was committed to replacing the GST rather than eliminating it. History shows that this was true only up to a point. While Chretien was careful with his words during the '93 campaign, he never corrected the media's claims that the Liberal Party wanted to scrap the tax which the Tories had introduced in 1990; a tax that the public loved to hate. Chretien therefore let stand the perception many voters had that a Liberal government would abolish the GST. Lawrence Martin said the Liberals "overplayed their hand" and that "[i]n the enthusiasm of trying to reach out to voters, they made it sound like they were burying the GST, not replacing it."[14] Edward Greenspon and Anthony Wilson-Smith noted, "Canadians remembered the rhetoric" and that "they hadn't heard the word 'harmonization' a lot."[15]

When the GST issue resurfaced in 1996, columnist Jeffrey Simpson said "the Liberal Party misled" the public "not in the vague words in the party's Red Book but in the multiple pronouncements of Liberal candidates and MPs before and during the election about scrapping, abolishing and killing the tax."[16] In another column, Simpson said that if the Liberals were "interested in honesty, even of the political variety, they would have outlined something to replace the GST."[17] Terence Corcoran, then Simpson's colleague at the *Globe and Mail*, admitted the Red Book *said* the Liberals would replace the GST but that "[m]any Canadians ...were led to believe that the Liberal position on the GST was much stronger, that the tax would be abolished, buried, scrapped."[18]

During the 1993 campaign, Sheila Copps told an October 18 CBC-TV townhall meeting, "if the GST is not abolished I will resign." In early

1996 Copps, then deputy Prime Minister and Heritage Minister, vowed again to resign if the GST was not scrapped. As budget day approached, it became clear the government was not delivering what the public thought it had been promised. Martin was moving toward the harmonization of the federal GST with provincial consumption taxes. He apologized for not keeping the Red Book promise but said it was the only workable solution. He wanted his apology to be stronger, but Chretien maintained that Martin's actions had actually fulfilled the Red Book promise of replacing the GST.

John Nunziata, a Liberal MP from Toronto, along with Copps, Don Boudria and Brian Tobin, most of them members of the celebrated Rat Pack that dogged Mulroney in the mid-'80s, signaled they didn't think Chretien's legalistic explanation and Martin's apology cut it. Nunziata publicly criticized the government, and Chretien responded by booting him out of the caucus. During debate in Question Period, the government was dancing around the issue, attempting to explain that it had fulfilled the Red Book promise. Meanwhile, broadcast media replayed Copps' 1993 campaign promise to resign if the GST was not abolished. She would try to evade responsibility by pleading that "a fast-lip comment in the course of an election campaign should not put me in a position of having to resign." She went so far as to joke that she offered her resignation to the Prime Minister in the House of Commons on a note that said, "I resign" which, of course, was not accepted. The Prime Minister even shared the note with his colleagues, passing it to them, like schoolchildren, in Parliament.[19]

Neither the public nor the press appreciated the humour and soon thereafter Copps resigned from the House of Commons with a caveat; she would run immediately to regain her seat in a $500,000 by-election. Chretien did not think she needed to resign, as he defiantly maintained that the government had kept its GST promise. Chretien was also proud of the fact that his government had not lost a Cabinet minister to scandal and he was particularly sensitive to the idea of losing one over the growing GST debacle. The Prime Minister wanted to fight, to beat the rap that he had broken a promise.[20] Copps eventually said that she had to do the honourable thing and resign her seat, but as the *Globe and Mail*'s Jeffrey Simpson scathingly noted at the time, her resignation was "a spectacular example of externally imposed honour." The fact was, the pressure to step down was great and she did, in fact, fight the idea that she should resign for nearly a month. As Simpson said, Copps sat at the Cabinet meeting when the government decided not to eliminate the GST and she didn't resign. When the government announced that it wasn't scrapping the GST she didn't resign. The opposition parties, listeners to radio call-in shows, editorial writers (including those at the *Toronto Star*), even her own constituents (she was booed at Copps Coliseum when she accompanied Prince Charles) all denounced her duplicity.[21] And it was only after all that uproar that she decided to do "the honourable thing."

In a cynical ploy, Copps stepped down and was immediately re-elected. Hamilton East returned the incumbent to office leading *Toronto Sun* editorial cartoonist Andy Donato to draw Hamilton voters as a bunch of butt heads. Copps, like the Liberal Party, would not suffer terribly for promises that had been broken.

But even according to the standard that Chretien said he should have been held to – merely replacing the GST – the government fell short. Although the consumption taxes of the Atlantic Provinces and the federal government were eventually harmonized, there was still no national re-working of the tax. Chretien blamed Ontario Premier Mike Harris, who initially signaled support for harmonization but whose eventual refusal to consider it sank any chances of getting the other provinces to sign on. Michael Bliss said Chretien got as much HST cooperation as he did because "Three Liberal dependencies in Atlantic Canada harmonized."[22]

Replacing the GST was not the only broken promise from the Red Book. A key element of Chretien's campaign was the appointment of an independent ethics commissioner. After the scandals of the Mulroney era, Chretien tapped into the country's dissatisfaction with the unaccountable and sometimes corrupt goings-on in Ottawa. He said he wanted an ethics commissioner with teeth. Under a Liberal regime, according to Chretien's '93 campaign promise, the ethics counselor would answer to Parliament. The Red Book said an independent ethics counselor "will report directly to Parliament." However, even after more than a decade in power, Chretien never appointed a truly independent ethics commissioner.

As scandal after scandal broke, Howard Wilson, the Prime Minister's ethics counselor, almost always ruled in favour of the Liberal Party and its leader.

Wilson was in the unenviable position of investigating and ruling upon apparent improprieties, while being answerable only to the Prime Minister. Indeed, Wilson's job was dependent upon Chretien's goodwill. With hardly a reason, Chretien could remove Wilson from the job. Why upset his boss? It was clear that when Wilson "investigated" conflict of interest charges against Cabinet ministers or the Prime Minister, he had a conflict of interest of his own.

Wilson would prove to be a reliable ally to Chretien as the endless litany of scandals broke. Chretien would trumpet Wilson's findings to exonerate himself. The result, however, "left the ethics counselor looking like a prime-ministerial poodle,"[23] a toothless lapdog instead of a watchdog.

David Zussman, an advisor to Chretien, later recalled that the Prime Minister eschewed the independent ethics commissioner because its anticipated costs were outweighed by the benefits. Zussman, who approximated the cost to $10 million at the time, said, "It would be like creating a new privacy commissioner or information commissioner."[24] The decision not to fulfill this Red Book promise was made in the first few months of Chretien's tenure. Chretien argued that an ethics counselor, that is, an advisor, would suffice, and that ultimately the Prime Minister should be held responsible for the ethics of members of his Cabinet.

The first "ethics" test for the Liberals came in October 1994 when Heritage Minister Michel Dupuy was discovered to have contacted the Canadian Radio-Television and Telecommunications Commission on behalf of a radio station owner in his riding. Chretien accepted Dupuy's excuse that it was an honest mistake. The Opposition quite reasonably thought Dupuy to be in a conflict of interest because as Heritage Minister, Dupuy oversaw the CRTC. After sustained pressure from the opposition, Chretien referred the case to his ethics commissioner. Wilson, predictably, found nothing wrong, a judgment that would be frequently repeated in the years to come.

Furthermore, the way Chretien handled that mini-scandal was a sign of things to come. First, he denied that it was a problem. A Prime Minister who does not acknowledge ethical problems within his Cabinet does not have to publicly deal with them. More importantly, however, was the way Chretien told Parliament he handled it; his explanation had raised suspicions that the Prime Minister was less than truthful in his handling of this ethics file.

The Dupuy scandal, while not major, foreshadowed how Chretien would deal with other, more serious improprieties; in this instance, as in many others that would follow, the Prime Minister first diminished the significance of the wrongdoing. And it seems clear that he sought the advice of his ethics counselor, Howard Wilson, *after* he had decided how to handle the minister in question and only after relentless pressure from the Opposition created the need to be seen to be doing something about the issue. Chretien would always stick by his Cabinet ministers. As Lawrence Martin observed, contrasting Chretien to Mulroney's swift response to erring Cabinet members, "Chretien would show no such decisiveness, preferring to dodge, dilly-dally and stonewall."[25]

It soon came to light that four other Cabinet ministers had contacted the CRTC over applications. Chretien again decided to excuse their conduct: "I have said before that this government will make mistakes, but they will be honest mistakes and we will always move to correct them."[26]

Wilson had another Cabinet minister to deal with during Chretien's first term. In 1996, Ethel Blondin-Andrews, the Youth Minister, used government credit cards during personal vacations in Hawaii and Mexico. She admitted using them to pay for car rentals but added that she paid them back. She also used a government credit card for a $554.53 down payment on a fur coat. She excused herself because she repaid the money and, anyway, the fur coat was to show "solidarity" with native fur trappers: "It's important to me as an aboriginal representative."[27]

Wilson's response to this tasteless imbroglio was understated: "I told her it would be better to use her own card."[28]

It was obvious that the ethics counselor was a lapdog and that even if the office had more teeth, Wilson would never do more than utter approving little peeps.

There were numerous other promises that Chretien failed to keep, including tackling Canada's chronically high unemployment rate and re-negotiating NAFTA. On unemployment, the Liberal government offered no program and over time, the rate fell steadily. This is defensible but it was hardly in keeping with a 1993 campaign promise.

In fact, this was an issue over which the Liberals ridiculed outgoing Prime Minister Kim Campbell, who said that unemployment was likely to remain high no matter who won the election. As for NAFTA, the Liberals did not renegotiate the deal, in part because Chretien wanted to foster a close relationship with Bill Clinton, who had expressed no interest at all in a new agreement. Over time, Chretien even became an advocate of expanding trade.

After the intense and very public criticism over breaking of Red Book promises, particularly on the GST and the independent ethics counselor, Chretien released a document entitled "A Record of Achievement: A Report Card on the Liberal Government's 36 Months in Office." Speaking before the biennial meeting of the Liberal Party on the third anniversary of the party's '93 election to power, Chretien bragged that his government had kept 78 per cent of their Red Book commitments. He said his government's record of keeping better than three-quarters of its promises was "not exactly a bad score." He added that "A Record of Achievement," which maintained that the Liberals kept 153 of 197 promises, was, like his government, "no bells, no whistles, no bull." He claimed the document set "a new standard of accountability on the part of a party in office." Regarding the GST, "A Record of Achievement," said it was "a work in progress." But the other broken promises were not insignificant. As the *Toronto Star* reported, the list included, among others, "the government's failure to provide stable funding for the CBC, to create 50,000 new child-care spaces and to double to $11 billion funding for research and development."[29] Defending their failure to deliver on all their promises, especially the most expensive ones, Chretien and Paul Martin blamed federal finances that were worse than they anticipated when the Red Book was first drafted. The *Star*, however, noted that during the '93 campaign, Chretien said he would not use that excuse for failing to deliver on his promises.

Blaming larger than expected deficits is a common excuse by new governments, but Chretien also offered another, rather novel explanation. In May of 1996, shortly after Sheila Copps resigned her seat, Chretien said, "Sometimes in the course of a mandate, you are faced with a situation where you cannot deliver. You have to have some flexibility in the administration because of acts of God that come in the administration." In the case of the 50,000 new childcare spaces, the "act of God" that Chretien was referring to was the refusal of provinces to pay half the costs of the program. That would be more accurately described as an act of politicians rather than an act of God.[30]

The Canadian Election Survey (1997) found that Chretien would benefit "from voters' short memory"[31] as polling results showed that few voters recalled the Liberal Party's commitment to create jobs or too much of anything else that had been in the Red Book.

* * * * * *

Halfway through the first term came the most serious challenge to Chretien's leadership, and indeed to Canada's existence: the sovereignty referendum in Quebec. Historian Michael Bliss said that on the night of October 30, 1995, "Canada almost collapsed." Long before the fateful referendum, it was apparent that the government had no national unity strategy. The Liberal government's response was nothing more than continuing the long tradition of chequebook federalism, a policy that never bought the loyalty of Quebecers. During the 1994 provincial election, 13 months before the referendum, the federal government offered a package of goodies[32] that included a $140 million labour training agreement, money for pilot projects for one-stop government services, $4.8 million for Montreal's botanical gardens, the establishment in Montreal of the office of Commission for Environmental Cooperation, $27 million for a convention centre in Quebec City (despite the fact the province refused to sign up with the

infrastructure program that funded it) and $380 million in additional
equalization payments.[33] All this and more was meant to demonstrate
to the province that if it re-elected Liberal premier Daniel Johnson, it
could count on the continued generosity of Ottawa. Meanwhile,
Canadians were getting tired of the unity debate; in the previous 15
years they had suffered through a close separation vote in Quebec,
seemingly endless constitutional debates, the election of the separatist
Bloc Quebecois as the Official Opposition in Ottawa, and relentless
and repeated threats from separatist governments in Quebec City. Still,
many Canadians found Chretien's apparent indifference to the
referendum to be an invitation to a constitutional crisis. The Canadian
Press' Joan Bryden reported, "Commentators have begun complaining
the federal government has no strategy to advance the federalist cause
despite polls suggesting the Parti Quebecois is poised to win the
election expected this fall."[34] Bryden wondered if Chretien's "'don't
worry, be happy' assurances that Canada will survive" had "lulled
Canadians into a false sense of security."

Chretien was so confident of a federalist victory that he apparently
wasn't concerned about the outcome of the provincial election.[35]

Oddly, the Johnson government never trumpeted Chretien's policy of
chequebook federalism, so many Quebecers never became aware of
the favours being lavished upon them. Johnson continued to bash
Ottawa. Chretien was never seen to be an ally and on September 12,
1994, the province elected Jacques Parizeau and the Parti Quebecois
to power with 77 of 125 seats.

The Chretien plan was to deal with the threat of separation when the
possibility of Quebec leaving Canada was imminent. He was roundly
criticized for not trying to prevent it before it became a serious likelihood.
In the weeks before the referendum vote, Canadians worried that the
province might break apart from Canada. The Prime Minister was

noticeably absent during the campaign. This is in stark contrast to Jean Chretien's barnstorming across *la belle Province* in 1980 in the first separation referendum.

On October 30, 1995, Quebec narrowly voted against sovereignty. Many in the media thought that a public demonstration from out-of-province Canadians in Montreal was what turned the tide. Many Canadians, even to this day, remember the huge Canadian flag that was paraded through the streets of Montreal, and there is still considerable opinion both inside and outside Quebec that it was this demonstration which tipped the *non* side to the slightest – 50.6 per cent to 49.4 per cent – victory. Some political observers said that it was the passionate federalism of then federal Progressive Conservative leader Jean Charest that kept Canada together. But on the evening of the vote, after the federalist victory became clear, Chretien pre-empted Charest's speech. John Crispo, professor emeritus at the Joseph L. Rotman School of Management at the University of Toronto, said that as yesterday's man in Quebec, Chretien was "pathologically jealous" of Charest and vindictively prevented him from appearing on television screens that evening. He also perhaps inadvertently hurt Charest's chances of winning the provincial election in 1998 after the former Tory leader became the leader of the Liberal Party in Quebec.[36] Chretien's ploy of doing nothing was either calculatingly brilliant or just plain lucky. Bliss said that given how close the federalist win was, "Chretien and his advisors proved to have been recklessly complacent in the run-up to the vote."[37]

Either way, there seems to be a connection between Chretien's unparalleled arrogance and conceit and his continued popularity in his home province. The two realities seem almost symbiotic. Former Tory MP Heward Grafftey says in his book *Democracy Challenged: How to End One-Party Rule in Canada*, that Chretien often boasted that he had won seven elections in Quebec, and most of them in difficult circumstances.[38] Could the fact that Chretien always just pulled off a victory have led him to believe that the *non* side in the referendum would win simply because *it was his side*? Such arrogance would be unpardonable in any other circumstance, but it seemed typical for this Prime Minister.

Within two years of the narrow federalist win, there was a national election. As the authors of the book *Unsteady State* observe, "considering the near-fiasco in the Quebec referendum on sovereignty, it is truly remarkable that so few Canadians were deeply dissatisfied with the Liberals about the national-unity issue" in that subsequent vote.[39] In other words, the Liberals paid no price for Chretien's apparently lax attitude on the national unity file.

There were several rather run-of-the-mill scandals that the Chretien government had to deal with in its first term in office, most of which emanated not with any original Liberal wrong-doing but which became problems because of the way the government handled them; specifically the Somalia affair and the Krever Report.

The Somalia cover-up is a bizarre chapter from the first term of the Chretien government, one that began before the Liberals even came to power. In early 1993, Prime Minister Brian Mulroney sent the Canadian Airborne Regiment Battle Group to Somalia under the auspices of the United Nations to restore peace and deliver humanitarian relief to the impoverished people in the East African nation. On March 4, members of an Airborne Group platoon killed a Somali thief. Subsequently, it took six weeks before the military began investigating the shooting. On March 16, a 16-year-old captive, Shidane Abukar Arone, was tortured and killed. By October, four members of the Airborne Group were convicted of various crimes. After Chretien assumed power, the CBC would report that records relating to the case were altered; in 1995, the CBC aired videos of hazing rituals at the Airborne's Canadian base in Petawawa, Ontario. Defence Minister David Collenette promptly disbanded the Airborne Group and set up an independent, three-person Commission of Inquiry.

The Inquiry into the Deployment of the Canadian Forces to Somalia was established and charged with looking at not just the Shidane Arone murder, but more broadly at the culture within the military to determine if that culture somehow increased the likelihood of such incidents. It was soon discovered that further records were altered or destroyed. The Canadian Defence Headquarters ordered serving personnel not to co-operate with the inquiry until they cleared what they were going to say with the Chief of the Defence Staff. Although the initial event took place during the Mulroney era, the alleged cover-up occurred during the Chretien regime, from 1993-1995.

The inquiry clearly became an annoyance to the government. Chretien complained that the inquiry was taking too long, saying that even Watergate was "settled in six or seven weeks." (In fact, the Senate investigation of Watergate took 20 months.[40]) Collenette was forced to defend allegations of paper shredding in the Department of National Defence. But instead of taking responsibility or even just clearly explaining what happened, Collenette saw anti-government conspiracies, criticized the Commission for taking media reports too seriously, and complained about the length of time the commission was taking to investigate.

The Opposition called for the resignations of Collenette and Chief of Defence Staff, General Jean Boyle. Because of the Prime Minister's comments about the excessive length of time the inquiry was supposedly taking, Preston Manning also charged that Chretien was "getting pretty close to participating in the cover-up by the military." Critics of the government called upon it to just let the inquiry do its job. In October 1996, Collenette resigned, not due to the pressure he was accused of placing on the commission, but because of a letter he had written to the Immigration and Refugee Board on behalf of a constituent. His resignation from Cabinet was temporary – he would return after the 1997 election – but it's worth noting that he left for a relatively minor breach of ministerial ethics, the kind of breach for which other Cabinet ministers would easily be forgiven.

Peter Desbarats, dean of the Graduate School of Journalism at the University of Western Ontario, was named a commissioner of the inquiry. He kept a journal that later became a best-selling book, *Somalia Cover-up: A Commissioner's Journal*. On October 4, the day Collenette resigned, Desbarats said journalists (and presumably himself) were skeptical of the reason Collenette offered. "The discovery of the letter," Desbarats writes, "allows Collenette to resign over a relatively minor matter, leaving the door open for an early return to cabinet, perhaps even before the election expected next spring."[41] As Preston Manning later put it, accepting the Defence Minister's resignation over some dubious and often tolerated infraction of Cabinet ethics rules – Michel Dupuy did the exact same thing and was defended by the Prime Minister for just doing what MPs do – allowed Chretien "to get Collenette out of the kitchen without accepting blame for the fire."[42]

Doug Young, who had served variously as Minister of Transportation and Human Resources, replaced Collenette. Hugh Segal said he was "unconstructively and excessively partisan and pugnacious."[43] Collenette described their contrasting styles: "We both play hardball," he said. "The difference is that I am a bit more clinical in the way I disembowel people."[44]

The first "disemboweling" was of General Boyle. He was immediately forced to resign – "to fall on his own sword" for the sake of the government – over, in Desbarat's estimation, a relatively minor infraction; Boyle had given an altered but "relatively innocuous" document to a journalist.[45] Boyle had been named Chief of Defence staff in January 1996 to re-establish control of the Defence Department and clear up the Somali scandal. However, in August, he testified before the Commission that he was responsible, as Assistant Deputy Minister of Defence for Policy and Communications in 1993, for releasing some altered documents on the Somalia file to CBC journalist Michael McAuliffe. *London Free Press* columnist Rory Leishman said, "Boyle confessed to having broken at least the spirit, if not the letter, of the Access to Information Act."

Boyle also admitted that since becoming the Chief of Defence staff earlier that year, hard copies of reports regarding the Airborne Regiment's Somali mission had been destroyed. Leishman said, "Here we have not a smoking gun, but a belching military cannon."[46] It took two months for Boyle to resign.

Soon after, both the Prime Minister and Defence Minister pressured the Commission to wrap up its proceedings. In his first days as Minister of Defence, Young had publicly indicated he wanted the inquiry to report by spring.

Desbarats lamented not just Chretien's comments about the slowness of the inquiry but his inability to defend himself or the proceedings. To do so would have been a political act, something Desbarats correctly thought to be inappropriate for anyone associated with the inquiry.[47]

On September 16, 1996, Chretien criticized the inquiry for the slow pace of the investigation. He did not mention that a primary reason for the slowness was the lack of cooperation from the military. Desbarats noted in his journal two days later, "Although we are not a court, we are a semi-judicial body that must remain independent of political influence." At least this Commissioner felt that comments coming from the government were undue political influence.

In mid-October, Chretien again criticized the length of the proceedings. Desbarats notes, "Chretien went further than he should have in criticizing our inquiry for taking so long." He continues: "Liberals had hoped originally that we would be finished long before the 1997 general election." He adds that despite the political pressure, "everyone knows that it will continue through the election campaign," and probably with great embarrassment to both the Liberal and Progressive Conservative parties.[48]

The government continued its criticism of the pace of the proceedings. Young went to the CBC and once again connected the timing of the inquiry's report to the election:"Certainly [we] wouldn't want to be in an election campaign with the inquiry still going on, having people telling me that I'm trying to cover something up." When asked what was more important, a speedy trial or proper inquiry, Young responded, "It's very important for me to end the inquiry."[49] Desbarats described the comments as, if not crossing the line, dangerously "treading a thin line between urging efficiency on us and appearing to want to close us down to prevent political embarrassment." Young's linking of the inquiry report and the election campaign, Desbarats said, brought "political considerations across the barrier that separates and insulates us from government interference."[50]

By mid-November, the Privy Council Office, which had oversight of the inquiry (through its control of the inquiry's purse-strings), began to exert pressure to get the report over and done with.[51]

Of course, Chretien could have waited for the inquiry to release its findings instead of calling an early election. But the government was seen to be putting undue pressure on the commission and to be doing so for political reasons. This was unlike the Airbus affair, in which the government led former Prime Minister Brian Mulroney through an agonizingly protracted legal battle because it claimed it did not want to interfere in a police investigation into the matter. In the case of Somalia, the government clearly tried to intervene in the inquiry process.

Suddenly, but not unpredictably, on January 10, 1997, Young declared that the inquiry was to complete its hearings within three months – just before an expected election call – and report by June, just after the election was completed. It was only the third time in Canadian history that an independent inquiry was shut down by the government, although this closure was substantively different than the other two.[ii.]

The Liberals got away with the political interference because, as Lawrence Martin notes, "it was not an issue ... that caught fire with Canadians," a fact the PMO knew from its own polling.[52] At the time, Desbarats thought Canadians did not understand how Young's decision would prevent the commissioners from properly investigating the incident and the alleged cover-up and, as a result, call into question the Commission's (and thus the government's) ability to implement meaningful reforms. Furthermore, he found that the media had done a poor job explaining these facts to the public. Also, the public was "tired of bad news" and Young's call for moving on played well.[53]

The irony is that the original investigation was about misbehaviour by the military under Mulroney, but the military's cover-up and the political attempt to hide that, could have dogged the Liberals during the election. But, in all likelihood, it wouldn't have. Years after the inquiry an unnamed PMO official told Lawrence Martin that the closure of the inquiry was probably unnecessary. Desbarats himself

---

ii. When judged against Liberal leaders of the past, Chretien was certainly a do-nothing prime minister. In both cases, inquiries into policy-related issues, not an investigation of an alleged impropriety, were closed down when the government changed hands. Never before had a government shut down its own inquiry and in neither earlier occasion was it intended to thwart the effort to get to the truth of an issue. (Peter Desbarats, "Somalia Cover-Up: A Commissioner's Journal", p. 269.)

wondered about the efforts to pressure the inquiry. He told Martin, "The fact that Chretien was willing to tamper with something like an independent inquiry for the sake of what appeared to be miniscule political advantage, I just thought, wow, if he'll do that, he'll do anything."[54]

What never made sense was Chretien's willingness to go to the mat over so little. Chretien and his Minister(s) of Defence seemed to be covering for top civil servants in the Defence Department. One such civil servant was Robert Fowler, a figure central to the scandal at the Department. He was appointed to the United Nations directly from his Defence posting. Columnist Diane Francis wrote that Chretien "spirited [him] out of the country to a plum job" and muses that he had done so because "Fowler's sister is married to Governor General Romeo LeBlanc, who happens to be one of Jean Chretien's best friends." She added, "[i]t certainly appears the boys look after the boys."[55]

As is often the case, the scandal that ensued was over suspicion of the cover-up and not the initial wrongdoing, which in this case, was something that had actually taken place on the previous government's watch.

It would not be the last time an inquiry into the previous government's business would lead to serious bungling by the Liberal government. In 1993, Brian Mulroney's government established a public inquiry to determine what, if anything, could have been done to protect the Canadian blood supply from HIV/AIDS and Hepatitis C. The "Inquiry on the Blood System in Canada", better known as the Krever Inquiry after its Commissioner, Justice Horace Krever, was to determine if Canada's blood supply was "as safe as it could be and whether the blood system [was] sound enough that no future tragedy will occur." An estimated 20,000 Canadians contracted Hep C from 1986-1990 because the Red Cross did not employ any screening system when collecting blood. The government wanted to know why not. The inquiry was sailing along smoothly until evidence surfaced that problems with the blood supply began as early as 1982. As Preston Manning notes, Chretien's government was "anxious to 'get at the truth' so long as the blame for the tainted-blood scandal could be attached to the previous Conservative government and the Red Cross." But when "Krever intended to name names and assign responsibility, the Chretien government's enthusiasm for truth seeking suddenly vanished."[56]

Once again, the Liberals attempted to intervene and affect the outcome of an independent inquiry. The government went to court in a desperate bid to restrict Krever's investigation, and in particular, the scope of what he would be allowed to say in his final report.

In the public's mind, the worst crime was the seeming indifference of the Chretien Liberals toward the tainted blood scandal's victims. The government upset many victims by arbitrarily deciding that only those who contracted diseases from infected blood between 1986 and 2000 would qualify for financial compensation from the federal government.[iii] Perhaps as many as 20,000 Hepatitis C victims were shut out of the $1.1 billion compensation package. Ontario Premier Mike Harris wrote to the Prime Minister protesting the arbitrary cut-offs, noting that the Krever Commission did "not support restricting assistance to only the 1986-1990 victims."

For two years, until 1997, the Chretien government frustrated the Krever inquiry's on-going investigations.

On April 28, 1998, the Reform Party introduced a motion in Parliament calling on the government to compensate equally all victims who contracted Hepatitis C through Canada's blood system. Many Liberal

---

iii. The Chretien government claimed that the dates had significance: before 1986, they said, there was no sure-fire test. By 1990, measures were in place to protect the integrity of the blood supply.

backbenchers agreed with the principle but the government called the whip and forced Liberal MPs to vote against the motion. It was defeated 154-137, with the Liberals voting as a block to ensure the outcome.

It was hardly the first time – and certainly would not be the last time – that the government forced Members of Parliament to tow the party line; what Lawrence Martin calls "trained seal time."[57] But, as Preston Manning notes, there was something particularly tragic about putting party above principle this time. Manning recalls that the government "forced its backbenchers, many of whom agreed with the motion, to vote against what compassion and their own personal ethics told them was right." He notes that one of the 154 votes against the motion was Dr. Carolyn Bennett, the MP from St. Paul's and a supporter of the rights of Hep C victims. Manning said the MPs had to follow the leader so that "even the Hippocratic oath of a medical doctor to 'do no harm' was subjugated to the Liberal ethic of 'Do no harm to the party, no matter who else gets hurt'."[58]

Chretien's handling of the tainted blood compensation issue betrayed his big "L" and small "l" liberal credentials, the idea that he fought for the little guy and the disadvantaged. His Health Minister, Allan Rock, was forced to oppose the motion despite his sympathy for the victims. He considered resigning.[59] Chretien dismissed concerns about not compensating every victim by saying, "It's why we have a medicare system." Lawrence Martin said that this was one of the many times that Chretien's "insensitive and heartless behaviour" would "dumbfound" those who often saw him "stand up for small people and their values."[60] These scandals were important less for the wrong-doing they expose than for their symbolism; they show how Chretien and the Prime Minister's Office would almost instinctively react to potentially embarrassing situations with a shell of stubbornness, self-interest, and self-protection.

Another scandal in the first term was the Airbus Affair in which it seems very likely that the government leaked details of an RCMP investigation to smear the name of former Prime Minister Brian Mulroney. The timing of that leak, wherever it came from, was also a boon to the Liberals in that the story managed to deflect voters' attention away from the near disastrous outcome of the Quebec referendum.

In the weeks immediately following the October 1995 referendum, a letter written by a government official to a Swiss Bank was leaked to the press. The *Financial Post* reprinted a letter signed by Justice Department lawyer Kimberly Prost to Swiss authorities, indicating that Mulroney himself was linked to allegations of favouritism and possible kickbacks involving the $1.8 billion purchase of 34 Airbus A-320 airplanes by Air Canada in 1988. The RCMP had investigated the deal at the time but closed the file.

The Justice Department letter appeared to confirm what the CBC's *fifth estate* reported in March 1995, that Progressive Conservative insiders used their influence within the government to deliver the deal and that in the process they gained financially. But there was never any hint that Mulroney was himself involved in criminal activity until the *Financial Post* published the leaked letter eight months later. The letter claimed that German businessman Karlheinz Schreiber was given a commission by Airbus Industries to pay Mulroney and his friend, lobbyist and former Newfoundland Premier Frank Moores, to ensure Airbus got a piece of the action when Air Canada upgraded its fleet.

Mulroney filed a defamation suit against both the federal government and the RCMP, which had reopened the investigation. Rumours swirled that Mulroney had leaked the letter himself as part of a bizarre gambit to protect Moores, Schreiber and himself by making it practically impossible to proceed with the investigation. This would have had him in the fantastic circumstance of libeling himself, but that is precisely what the Liberals claimed. (For the record, *Financial Post* reporter Philip Mathias, who was the first to report on the leaked letter, denies that Mulroney was his source.)

None of this would have mattered much except several Cabinet ministers and members of the Prime Minister's Office took an unusual level of interest in the case. This led to considerable suspicion that the RCMP investigation into the Airbus scandal was politically motivated. Whether or not that was the case, Mulroney argued that Justice Minister Allan Rock, ministerial aide Cyrus Reporter, RCMP Commissioner Philip Murray and individuals in the PMO including Peter Donolo, the Director of Communications, and Eddie Goldenberg, a long-time advisor to Chretien, should have acted to limit the damage done by the leaked letter. Mulroney suspected that it was actually the PMO that did the leaking.

The Prime Minister and the PMO maintained that Chretien did not know of the letter. In fact, the government claimed that Rock, his staff and the PMO all kept themselves at arm's length from the investigation. Ditto for Herb Gray, who as Solicitor General oversaw the RCMP, had knowledge of the investigation and of the fact that Mulroney was a possible subject of that investigation. Gray claims to have never told Chretien, nor did he believe that he was obligated to tell him.[61]

In the meantime, as legal wrangling over the libel suit began, the RCMP investigation continued.

The libel case could have been settled early on with a formal retraction of the letter, an apology to Mulroney and repayment of his legal bills. But the government fought back and Mulroney demanded $50 million. During the trial, Mulroney made a request for a room for personal use during what was expected to be a lengthy trial. The government complained, and the press dutifully reported, that the former Prime Minister was making "imperial demands". But while the government and media made much ado about the "special treatment" Mulroney received, they both enjoyed similar privileges by being routinely granted rooms for their use during the trial.[62] It seemed petty that the government would attack Mulroney on this during the course of a trial, but such was the public relations battle.

After the trial began and things did not appear to be going the government's way, government lawyers became "desperate to settle."[63] Government negotiators agreed to a financial settlement that covered the legal and non-legal costs of the ordeal for Mulroney (but not the $50 million) and wrote a statement acknowledging that the allegations of wrong-doing "were – and are – unjustified." Lastly, there was an apology on behalf the government and RCMP for "any damage suffered by Mr. Mulroney and his family." Rock wanted to apologize publicly to Mulroney, saying the integrity of the investigative process had been restored and expressing his personal regret to Mulroney. But as William Kaplan reports in his *Presumed Guilty: Brian Mulroney, the Airbus Affair and the Government of Canada*, Chretien stopped him and forced the Justice Minister to send prepared remarks to the PMO for vetting.[64] Chretien biographer Lawrence Martin says that whatever Chretien's role was up to the point of the apology, he definitely made the decision that the government would not offer a sincere or heartfelt apology: "The Jean Chretien who would go to any extreme to avoid conceding defeat was alive and well."[65] Martin describes the apology as "grudging" and "mean-spirited," Rock's tone "not the least bit regretful" and "almost aggressive."[66]

The press criticized the government for apparent duplicity for apologizing to Mulroney for the letter's conclusion that Mulroney had acted improperly on the one hand and permitting the RCMP investigation to continue on the other. Rock said that the police decide "when to start and when to stop investigations" and indicated that there would be no further interference in the case. The press also criticized the government for taking so long to settle, thus costing taxpayers money on what seemed to be a delaying tactic.

Rock would later regret not offering a more thorough apology, but not until there was heat for the justice minister over his handling of the case. Chretien never felt the need to apologize. The Prime Minister claimed that Mulroney had only asked for an apology in January 1997. Mulroney however, asked for an apology from the beginning.

Mulroney told Kaplan that he thought the PMO leaked the letter from the Justice Department. Cynics might believe that the government leaked the letter – which sparked a fury of media coverage for weeks to come – in the aftermath of the close referendum, as a way of deflecting criticism of Chretien's do-nothing strategy on the national unity file. On the other hand, it may have been part of the on-going personal animosity between Chretien and Mulroney. Lawrence Martin concedes that if Chretien had been acting on a personal vendetta against the former Prime Minister, it would have been pointless. Pointless perhaps, but consistent with what Martin believes to be Chretien's fighting spirit. Factor in the half-apology and it is easy to conclude that, "the government really had been out to impugn the former Prime Minister."[67]

Kaplan says "the evidence is far from complete" as to whether Chretien knew about the letter before it was published in the *Financial Post*, "but what there is suggests, at the very least, that he knew something was up."[68] Considering that in mid-1995 Chretien told an Ottawa businessman in a conversation about Mulroney that he was considering calling a Royal Commission into the Airbus purchase, he must have known something was up. As Kaplan says, Chretien's "claim not to know anything about the investigation until the story broke in the *Financial Post* simply strains credibility."[69]

The RCMP investigation concluded, without further impugning of Mulroney, in 2003. Chretien was defiant in never acknowledging any wrongdoing against the former Prime Minister although when the case finally closed, Mulroney was vindicated of any criminal activity.

There would be no political price to pay. In the pantheon of recent political villains, few would challenge Mulroney for top-spot in the Canadian public's mind. There would be little sympathy for Mulroney, and the lingering taint of scandals from Mulroney's much-maligned government led the public to believe that he could be capable of such criminal activity. And, whether calculated or just by dumb luck, the Liberals once again got away with their shenanigans.

The episode is also an ugly and extreme example of the Chretien Liberals' propensity for destroying their opponents, for personalizing their political attacks and engaging in the ultimate "ad hominem" style of argumentation. In this case, though, it was utterly unnecessary. Their opponent was, in fact, a "former opponent". But it fits the pattern of character assassination that Chretien would use on the campaign trail against Reform leader Preston Manning and Canadian Alliance leader Stockwell Day.

The do-nothing government of the Liberals was an early sign of Chretien's arrogance. It sent a clear signal that Chretien cared more about having power than doing anything with it. The party under Chretien fell victim to the conceit that it was the Natural Governing Party and that even in the absence of a real agenda, it should govern. There is also the personal narcissism of the Prime Minister that, absent any real purpose for being in office, he should still be there anyway.

Furthermore, after the 1993 election, the Liberals did not feel they needed to do anything. The NDP barely retained official party status, the right was divided and the Tories practically eviscerated. With no opposition to challenge them to greater heights, the Liberals settled for getting by.

Historians J.L. Granatstein and Normal Hiller said the government had a "mixed record"[70] in its first term and that the record included a string of broken promises: GST, re-examining NAFTA, and establishing a new (and presumably better) level of ethics. Furthermore, Chretien misjudged the gravity of the threat of secession by Quebec, presided over the precipitous fall of the dollar and initiated a trade-inspired foreign policy that led Canada to ignore human rights abuses abroad. In international affairs, Canada's influence is barely felt, its commitment to soft power leading it to have "little to say to the world."[71]

The Liberals promised in 1993 to "save" Canada's social programs, but transfer payments to the provinces were cut to help cover health and education costs. They promised to cut unemployment but the change (from 11.2 per cent to 9.6 per cent) was relatively modest. Considering the priority the Liberals placed on the issue in 1993, the failure to deliver in a major way should have led Canadians to consider the lack of results on the jobs front a broken promise. But the Liberals were the beneficiaries of the public's collective short-term memory.

And the virtual amnesia that led Canadians to forget about or forgive broken promises also led them to forget the scandals that plagued the first term or forgive them as minor, pardonable and innocuous deficiencies or shortcomings. More importantly, however, what Chretien gave the country in his first term was a peek at how he would later deal with more serious Cabinet wrongdoings and with a scandal that would centre on him personally. In short, in the first term, we were witness to unbridled arrogance on the part of the Liberal Party; an arrogance that said standards of behaviour expected from Mulroney while the Liberals were in opposition would not apply to Chretien's government. In other words, as leader of the Natural Governing Party, the rules would not apply to Chretien or his government.

CHAPTER 3

VOTERS' SEAL OF APPROVAL?

I n early 1997, after slightly more than three years in power, there was a widespread expectation that the Chretien Liberals would go back to the public for another mandate. The party had won a strong majority in 1993, and while there was little reason for a return to the voting booth, the opinion polls seemed right. As Lawrence Martin explained it later, the most important reason to call an election was that the Liberals would probably retain nearly all of the 98 seats (out of 99) that they won in Ontario in 1993. Martin noted that David Smith, Chretien's campaign manager in Ontario, informed the prime minister that the time was right for another election campaign; "the essential ingredients of a win were there," Smith advised the Liberal leader.[72] Publicly, Chretien offered two reasons for going to the polls just 43 months into his government's mandate. First, the Prime Minister tried to claim that the government was in the fourth year of its mandate. While this was technically true, the conventional wisdom on these things would indicate that a four-year term fall close to the fourth anniversary of the previous election, not three-and-a-half years into the mandate. The second reason Chretien gave was that, now that the country's finances were in order, he wanted some direction and a mandate from the voters on what to do with future budgetary surpluses.

Chretien had done little in his first term. As Jeffrey Simpson has noted, the Prime Minister essentially had a "defensive agenda" of ensuring that Quebec did not separate and that the country's finances were put on a more solid footing.[73] But even these modest (read: safe) goals were not without consequence. Chretien's inaction was seen to contribute to a close referendum call that could have resulted in the disintegration of Canada. Also, Finance Minister Paul Martin began the process of cutting back spending and gutting programs that many Liberals and voters, especially in Atlantic Canada, had long cherished. There was not much of a record upon which to run. Still, he went to the polls, knowing that while he may not have excited Canadians they would settle for him. With a support base that was wide but not very deep, Chretien took his good poll numbers and the divided and weak opposition into an early and unnecessary election. As the government prepared for a spring election call floods ravished southern Manitoba as the overflowing Red River threatened small rural communities and parts of Winnipeg. Critics said that it was callous of the government to go through with a federal election while a portion of the country struggled to survive, rebuild their lives and make their livelihood. Aside from the perceived callousness of an unnecessary election based on political opportunism (the winnability factor in Ontario combined with the division on the right), there were questions of whether an election could be properly conducted under the disastrous conditions the floods imposed. Preston Manning requested that Section 13 of the Elections Act be invoked to postpone an election for three months in regions affected by natural disasters. Jean-Pierre Kingsley did not accept the Reform Party's argument that a flood made holding an election in the area "impractical" as outlined in the Act. Signs could be found in homes in the affected area that read, "Sandbag the Liberals."[74]

Come election day, however, Manitoba remained the most Liberal of the western provinces, although the party's numbers dropped significantly from 1993. They finished with six of 14 federal seats in the province, down from 12 in 1993. Still, Manitoba voters were forgiving, giving the Liberals more than one-third of the vote. By comparison, the NDP had four seats, Reform three and the Tories one. Furthermore, no other party garnered more than 24% of the vote. It appeared that the callous disregard for the voters in south central Manitoba cost the Liberals very little. A close look at the election results shows that after Ontario, Manitoba was the province where the division among the right wing parties helped the Liberals the most. The campaign proved that Chretien was out-of-touch with the concerns of the public. Chretien held a carefully orchestrated townhall meeting. This was in no way a public forum intended to give common citizens a chance to question the prime minister; the 13 questioners (out of more than 200 attending the event) were "pre-selected and even given a little coaching on how to put their queries."[75] Even with those seemingly favourable (and arguably rigged) conditions, he faced several tough questions that he did not handle eloquently, including one from a Saskatchewan woman with three university degrees who could still not find work. Chretien's response showed his common touch: "Some are lucky, some are unlucky." He elaborated: "I think you have to keep trying," and urged her to relocate to an area where there might be jobs. To another unemployed woman, a Nova Scotian, he suggested that she open a business and noted that interest rates were low. Even Chretien's sympathetic biographer, Lawrence Martin, called the performance "callous"[76]; His replies were feisty, resembling more an angry Parliamentary exchange than a question and answer with potential voters.

The defiance and aggressiveness toward the townhall participants appeared to be a symptom of Chretien's impatience and disgust with voters who simply refused to accept the notion that the Liberals were the Natural Governing Party. He seemed to approach the session with the notion that the Liberals were simply entitled to lead, and that he, the leader of this Party shouldn't have to be subjected to questions; how dare anyone question him or, by implication, cast doubt on his leadership? To the Chretien Liberals, the campaign – with events such as the townhall meeting – was merely a formality; a necessary evil leading up to a seal of approval from the country that would be nice to attain once again. But to the Liberals, the outcome was clearly never in doubt. While calling the election on the rationale that the government needed a mandate for a new direction in the deficit-cutting era it was about to embark upon, the Liberals offered few specifics about what they planned to do when re-elected. The '97 campaign could very well be called the Seinfeld election, a campaign about nothing.

The Canadian public recognized Chretien's cynicism and although his party continued to hold an insurmountable lead, the viability of the majority was eventually called into question. With a week to go, the party's pollster, Michael Marzolini of Pollara found that with its support waning in Atlantic Canada, the Liberals were headed for a minority government.[77] According to his calculations, the party would be reduced to five seats in the region and their majority status imperiled. On June 2, election day, the Liberals won just 11 of the 32 seats in the Maritimes; it hadn't turned out as badly as Marzolini had predicted. Atlantic Canada was probably the only region where Chretien's record made any difference in voting patterns in 1997. Paul Martin's cuts in transfer payments and reforms to unemployment insurance were felt the most keenly in this region because of its impoverished status and chronically high unemployment. The NDP and the PC's campaigned hard against these cuts in the Maritimes, and the Conservatives at least were rewarded for their efforts with enough seats to easily qualify for official party status once again.

* * * * * *

It was clear that the 1997 campaign was a cynical effort on Chretien's part based on dividing his political opponents and misrepresenting them to the voters. Before and during the campaign Chretien maintained that 50 per cent plus one in a Quebec sovereignty vote would not be enough to break up the country. That position clearly cost him votes in Quebec, leading even some federalist voters in that province away from the softer, distinct-society supporting, Jean Charest-led Tories, to back the Bloc Quebecois. It is noteworthy that this hard-line position against the threat of Quebec separatism was not part of Chretien's 1995 referendum strategy but was enunciated just before a federal election, where it was used to maximum political effectiveness, particularly in the rest of the country. Whatever the wisdom of the policy, Chretien appeared to adopt it for political reasons. It appeared to be part of a strategy described by Liberal advisor John Duffy as "the exploitation not so much of vote-splitting among right-wingers over ideology, as among Tories along regional lines."[78] Chretien also dismissed Reform as a western phenomenon and attacked Manning over his perceived extreme conservatism and anti-Quebec policies. Chretien raised the spectre of regional factionalism and, just 19 months after the close Quebec referendum, frightened Canadians about the possibility of re-opening constitutional debate and the unity question. The effect of such a campaign was to play centrist (and anxious) Central Canada and Western Canada against one another. Chretien made a calculated decision to keep the vast majority (if not all) of his Ontario seats and a smattering of urban Western seats knowing that the more conservative and anti-Ottawa West would never vote Liberal in significant numbers.

The national political debate over Quebec was meant less to sway Quebec voters than those in Ontario. Western voters tend to take a harder line on accommodating Quebec than Ontario voters do and thus Manning's preparation for the possibility of Quebec separating (the so-called Calgary Declaration) was criticized in Central Canada and used against the Reform Party in Ontario. Chretien's moderately tough line on Quebec, combined with his attacks on Manning, effectively painted the Reform leader as a threat to Canadian unity. Ironically, Chretien did this while usurping the principles of the Calgary Declaration, now called "Plan B"[iv.] for himself and claiming he had always supported it.[79] The media repeated Chretien's claim that Reform could not make any headway in Ontario. Sadly, once the press reports something often enough, the conventional wisdom becomes a reality. Reform's efforts to pick up seats in the most populous province ended with the party losing the only seat it had held. Vote splitting on the right had cost the conservative side of the ledger 28 seats.

It is interesting, although perhaps pointless, to speculate on whether a united right might have won those 28 seats. There is a case to be made, as Neil Nevitte *et al* do in *Unsteady State* (a book that examines the 1997 election based on the results of the Canadian Election Survey), that many Reform Party voters would not have supported a Progressive Conservative alternative and that few Tories would have voted Reform had the PCs not existed. According to data collected from the 1997 Canadian Election Study by the Institute for Social Research at York University, "the ideological hearts of Progressive Conservative voters and Reform voters are in different places."[80] Proof of that, according to the study, was that on seven of eight general "ideological dimensions" (that rates issues such as cynicism about government, free enterprise, attitudes toward Quebec, US-Canada relations and moral traditionalism), Reform Party voters were far to the right of Conservative voters[81] and that often "Conservatives appear to be ideologically closer to the Liberals than to their rivals on the right."[82] This would seem to be supported by the finding that the second choice of 44 per cent of Conservative voters outside of Quebec was the Liberal Party, compared to just 17.7 per cent who would have

---

iv. Plan B is the term given to clearly setting out the consequences of Quebec separating.

voted Reform (and 19.5 per cent who would have voted NDP).[83] The study raised serious doubt about the potential success of a Reform-Conservative merger.

Simply combining the Reform-PC vote against the Liberal vote is hardly an accurate indicator of what would have happened if there were only one centre-right alternative to the Liberals. The point is, there was more than one and it is impossible to know how voters would have behaved given another set of circumstances. But surely both parties lost support. The internecine battle for political control of the right had made both look childish and unprofessional. And just as surely, Chretien was eager to exploit the perception that his primary opposition was divided, fighting among itself, and not ready to govern.

While vote splitting *may* have helped produce the Liberal majority, it was hardly the whole story. The Chretien gamble to go to the polls early worked. He was re-elected with a majority, albeit a reduced one. Chretien only narrowly held onto power through the "triumph of the centre in Canadian political life" – the phenomenon a group of political scientists described first happening in 1993[84] and which would prove to be the key to Liberal electoral success for a decade.

The 1997 Canadian Election Study found that the Liberals won for four reasons: they had a larger core of supporters; voters were optimistic about the economy; the government was dealing with the deficit, an issue that was in vogue at the time; and Chretien was the most popular leader outside of Quebec.[85] The Liberals also won because, as the Canadian Election Survey demonstrated, nearly half of all voters (48 per cent) were satisfied with the status quo. The authors of the study, however, fail to differentiate between "satisfied" with and "settling for" the Liberals. It could very well have been a case of the public having a myopic Panglossian view that the Canada of Chretien's Liberals was the best of all possible worlds despite the mountain of evidence to the contrary. Canadians thought they had the best possible government available. And believing that to be so, perhaps less than being satisfied with the status of quo, *contra* the Canadian Election Survey, the Canadian public entrenched the political status quo.

In *Unsteady State*, the authors say that the '97 elections did not signal a "reversion to the pre-1993 party system" because the Tory "revival" was not really all that impressive. The authors dismiss the idea that the Tories "regained [their] status as the only logical challenger to the Liberals."[86] Jean Charest, now the leader of the federal PC party, continued to preach the fiction that his party was the only viable national alternative and that only his caucus was a legitimate government - in - waiting. But the fact is, the Tories only regained their official party status in the Commons by riding a wave of anti-Liberal resentment in Atlantic Canada and winning some close Quebec ridings where support for the Bloc had ebbed. They were virtually shut out in the West.

Many political observers thought the loss of 22 Liberal seats signaled a major change in Canadian politics. Peter C. Newman said, "In the 11 hours it took 15 million Canadians to cast their ballots, something profoundly significant happened."[87] Gordon Gibson, writing in the *Globe and Mail*, said the government had a "shaky" mandate.[88] The *Toronto Sun* editorialized that Chretien faced "a balkanized Parliament in which his own authority has been severely damaged."[89] The paper thought it "serve[d] these arrogant Grits right for cynically calling this unnecessary election only 3 1/2 years into their mandate, expecting to cakewalk to victory." The significance for the *Sun* was that Chretien proved he no longer had what it took to be Prime Minister. In fact, the editorial called upon him to resign.

Indeed, the Progressive Conservatives rebounded from near extinction, going from two to 20 seats, just behind the revitalized NDP

(21 seats). Both were regional parties – the Tories getting most of their seats in Atlantic Canada and another quarter of their seats in Quebec, the NDP in Atlantic Canada and its traditional base of support in pockets of Saskatchewan and BC. The separatist Bloc Quebecois again took the majority of seats in Quebec. The Reform Party grew significantly within the confines of its Western base and became the Official Opposition. But no party was viewed as a legitimate national threat to the Liberals and still none looked like a government-in-waiting; many Canadians viewed the NDP and Reform as ideologically extreme. The Bloc was clearly a regional party and Reform was considered such while the Tories were reduced to a regional rump.

Significantly, in the all-important battleground of Ontario, the Liberals won 101 of 103 seats. Of the two exceptions, one was former Liberal MP John Nunziata in York South Weston who had battled with his own party over its broken GST promise. Until another party could seriously contend with the Liberals for a majority of Ontario seats, the Liberal government was safe, even after a loss of 10 seats. They may have been deprived of a Parliamentary majority, but would still have more than twice as many seats as the Official Opposition.

The Liberal dominance in Ontario led to them being jokingly referred to as the Bloc Ontario – for a few days until the novelty wore off. The media did not consider this a significant development but rather more as a political curiosity that lent itself to a moderately clever description. So even though it was accurate, the description never really stuck. It is clear, however, that the electoral domination of Ontario by the Liberals was the key to their political success, providing two-thirds of the party's seats in Parliament.

The central importance of Ontario to the electoral success of the Liberals began in 1988 when half of its caucus had come from that province. In every election since, Ontarians formed the majority of its caucus, and the percentage of Liberals from Ontario increased in all three subsequent elections. West of Manitoba, the Liberals barely beat the NDP, holding nine seats to the NDP's eight. Counting Manitoba, the Liberals held 15 Western seats and the NDP 12. By comparison, the Reform Party held 60 and the Tories 1. One could say that the Liberals barely qualified as a national party. In fact, the case could credibly be made that the Liberals had actually become nothing more than a regional party themselves, the very term with which they were busy painting their opponents. The only difference was that their brand of "regionalism" gave them more electoral success because their geographic "region" happened to contain a third of the seats in Canada's Parliament.

With fully two-thirds of their seats after the 1997 election (and nearly two-thirds after the 2000 election, although we're getting ahead of ourselves here) coming from Ontario, the Liberals had become a regional party with just enough success elsewhere to retain not just the government, but a majority of the seats in Parliament. With Canada's Toronto-Ottawa-Montreal media axis, success in Ontario and Quebec meant that journalists would propagate the fiction that Liberal support was "national' in scope. Many of the journalists writing these opinions didn't have any vision of the country beyond that "golden triangle" of central Canada, and to them, a win in this region was tantamount to winning the entire country. But as the authors of *Rebuilding Canadian Party Politics* said, the reliance on Ontario to deliver the vast majority of their seats "undermined the Liberal's credibility as a national party."[90]

* * * * * *

So what lessons did the Liberals learn? First, that with a divided opposition on their right, especially in Ontario, there was no party that could possibly challenge for a majority of the seats. However, the divided right explains only so much, even in Ontario. Whereas the Liberals won 38 per cent of the vote nationally, they won 49 per cent of the vote in Canada's most populous province. Ontario voters made up 46 per cent of Liberal support across the country. Only in tiny Prince Edward Island and the Northwest Territories did the Liberals run ahead of their national vote (45 per cent and 44 per cent respectively). The *Globe and Mail*'s Robert Sheppard explained that Ontario fell "completely under the spell of mumbly old Jean Chretien and his band of non-entities."[91] Sheppard found this odd because the province did not surrender "its political diversity" during the Diefenbaker or Trudeau reigns despite the fact that both garnered huge majorities. Furthermore, Ontarians had just voted for three different majority governments at the provincial level (David Peterson's Liberals in 1996, Bob Rae's NDP in 1990 and Mike Harris' Tories in 1995), a sign of a "charming capriciousness" that did not translate to the federal level.[92] At the same time, Sheppard noted that just three days after the election, few voters, when asked, would even admit to voting Liberal, "as if Ontarians [were] embarrassed at being considered a region *comme les autres*."[93] Perhaps it was the embarrassment of rewarding such a corrupt and inept gaggle of Liberal MPs?

What did the Chretien Liberals learn from the 1997 election? Mostly that not doing anything with the power they won could pay political dividends. Indeed, their one accomplishment – reducing the deficit by cutting program spending and transfers to the provinces – cost them dearly in Atlantic Canada, where they went from 31 to 11 seats (winning none in Nova Scotia), losing two senior cabinet ministers, David Dingwall and Doug Young, in the process. Indeed, Atlantic Canada may have been the only part of Canada in which policy mattered. The NDP certainly gained seats in this poorest of regions but even at that, the Liberals beat the NDP in the popular vote in Atlantic Canada by a margin of 33 to 24 per cent.

However, as Sheppard correctly noted (in another column), while the Liberals were chastened, they still had a majority and one that was stronger than their four-seat margin would normally indicate.[94] One reason for that was that the battled-damaged Tories and NDP, their resources spent fighting an election, could be co-opted in tight votes as neither wanted the Liberals defeated on a confidence motion which might force them to fight another campaign hard on the heels of the 1997 vote. The other reason was that even having five people absent in one day the Liberals still held four more seats than the combined opposition. They were not likely to lose any votes, especially not a confidence vote.

Furthermore, Chretien handled the situation perfectly. Just as he dealt with ethical lapses by pretending they were not ethical lapses, he accentuated the positive to paint a reduced majority as a series of small victories. Ontario stayed Liberal. For the first time since 1957, the Liberals re-elected a sitting MP from Alberta (in fact, two of them – David Kilgour and Anne McLellan)[95], and the Bloc lost seats in Quebec, indicating that Canada was stronger with Chretien at the helm in Ottawa. Chretien ignored the fact that voters had turfed almost one-eighth of the Liberal caucus. That didn't matter; what did matter was that he had been re-elected. After this vote, some political observers thought that the chastened Liberals, holding onto a relatively slim majority, would run Parliament differently. Peter C. Newman claimed that the Liberals were re-elected, "but without the comfortable majority that would allow them to govern as they chose."[96] University of Montreal political scientist Jane Jenson said that with a four-seat majority, the Prime Minister's Office would have to practice greater control of the caucus, joking that Chretien "can't let anybody die or go to the bathroom."[97] Indeed, in the coming years, the growing power of the PMO would become all too apparent although that had less to do with the reduced majority than with the jealous hoarding of all the control, power, and influence it could muster. For all that the '97 election supposedly changed, as Gordon Gibson noted, the government was still "run by the same stale old Liberal warhorses."[98] In other words, being "punished" by the voters with another majority government, the Chretien Liberals were still the Chretien Liberals. They also realized, "that any challenge from the left can be discounted."[99] They were not very vulnerable to the NDP when it came to cutting Canada's cherished employment and social programs, including health and education, programs the Liberals vowed to defend and claimed to protect. They could continue to ignore important and historically "Liberal" issues and themes with immunity from political consequence.

The Liberals could have been vulnerable in 1997 after massive spending cuts, a slew of broken promises and an unemployment rate in which they had hardly made a dent, in spite of promises in 1993 to do precisely that. Canadian voters were upset enough with the Liberals to drastically cut their majority, but the anger was not focused on any one issue. Some were angry over the arrogance of having an unnecessary election just 43 months into the mandate, only because it looked like good timing for the Liberals to win. Others were angry that the government had little to show for the time it had been in power, and still others were upset with the party for showing almost no vision or program for the next three to five years in office. But the new government would hold onto power with a bare majority, winning 154 of 301 seats. Yet, nothing really changed. If anything, the Chretien Liberals only became more arrogant. Canadians either forgot or forgave the Liberals for their political sins in the preceding 43 months, and the party basically pulled off a democratic coup. The voters had given the democratic seal of approval to Liberal arrogance.

CHAPTER 4

SECOND MANDATE

C hretien's second mandate was equally uneventful when it came to debates about policy and the different views of where Canada should be headed as it approached the new millennium. When asked in 1998 about the lack of vision by the government, House Leader Don Boudria said, "Look at what we've done. We've created the new Nunavut territory, amended the Wheat Board Act, ended the Crow rate and signed the land mine treaty. What's visionary? I think people prefer a party that governs without causing trouble."[100] The remark is quite revealing: acting on ideals and principles to make a better country is considered "causing trouble" by the Government House Leader. Is there any clearer admission that the Chretien Liberals sought power for power's sake? The second term of Jean Chretien would see a lot of trouble; 1997-2000 was notable only for a series of scandals much worse than the government experienced in Chretien's first three-and-a-half years in office. The emblematic catchwords for the second term would be initials (APEC and HRDC) and another "gate" – "Shawinigate" after Chretien's hometown.

In November 1997, Vancouver hosted the Asia-Pacific Economic Cooperation summit meeting to discuss economic issues affecting the Pacific Rim nations in Asia and North America. Police clashed with anti-globalization protestors and human rights activists; television cameras not only caught the police using pepper spray against demonstrators, but against a CBC cameraman as well. Once the conference was over, the talk was all about the RCMP's handling of the protestors, not the expansion of free trade across the Pacific Rim.

Questions quickly arose about the aggressive police actions and whether the Prime Minister's Office had signaled to the RCMP to clamp down on "dissent." Lawrence Martin reported that three months before the APEC summit, Chretien told the RCMP that he didn't want any "distractions" (Martin's word) in Vancouver.[101] The police harassed peaceful protestors, including one law student who had simply erected signs that said "Free Speech," "Freedom," and "Democracy." Craig Jones was held for 14 hours for this "crime" but eventually was released without charge, lending credence to the argument that the police were acting to suppress peaceful demonstrations, not maintain safety. Jean Chretien would say when asked about the use of pepper spray by police, "Pepper? That's something I put on my plate." It was classic Chretien: an insensitive quip about a serious situation, the gravity of which the Prime Minister either did not understand or did not care about. For someone who had electoral success for more than three decades, Chretien was growing increasingly out of touch. Chretien later told the nation, "So I made a joke … Relax a bit." Martin said the "remark made the story bigger than it might otherwise have been." But if the story wasn't "big" it wasn't because the events surrounding the APEC summit were insignificant, Rather,it was because the media and the public seemingly could not be bothered about ideas and principles central to democracy. Indeed, as numerous essays in *Pepper in Our Eyes: The APEC Affair* make abundantly clear, serious constitutional, rule of law and liberty issues were raised by the role, if any, played by the PMO in what happened between the RCMP and protestors at the summit.[102] As contributor Andrew D. Irvine noted, the involvement of the PMO in security arrangements may seem "innocent enough" but "if the PMO attempted to have the RCMP suspend the rights of protestors without compelling security reasons for doing so, this clearly crossed the line between legitimate political involvement and improper political interference."[103] Lawyer Donald J. Sorochan makes the same point, wondering "whether the federal government inappropriately used the RCMP for political purposes rather than the enforcement and preservation of peace."[104]

Much of what happened is clouded by fog that could have been cleared by a proper inquiry and cooperation from the PMO. But due to the normal operating procedures of the Chretien PMO, little light was shone on the controversy: did the Prime Minister or his staff order police to suppress the fundamental rights of Canadians to free speech and free association? The answer, even now, remains unclear.

What is known is that Indonesian dictator Raden Suharto requested that protestors not embarrass him and numerous heads of state made it clear that they wanted security measures beefed up. Contrary to the usual practice, the government allowed Suharto's guards to carry guns while protecting the Indonesian leader in Canada. A charitable interpretation of these events might be that the PMO signaled to the RCMP that they should prevent a direct showdown between protestors and Indonesian security personnel with the intent of avoiding an embarrassing situation in which foreign armed guards might end up shooting at Canadian protestors.

Chretien and staff strain credibility by denying that they ordered the RCMP actions. Despite their denials, W. Wesley Pue says there was "a document trail that became public [which] clearly showed deep political involvement in policing arrangements."[105] At the very least, the Prime Minister's people left the impression with the police that protests could be squelched. The PMO noted in a memo that they had "concerns about the security perimeter at UBC," where the summit was held, "not so much from a security point of view but to avoid embarrassments to APEC leaders."[106] Student protestors reported that police said they had orders from the PMO that there be "no signs and no people" near the motorcade of leaders. Pue also reports that audiotapes of police transmissions "were punctuated with 'Jean Carle wants this' and 'Jean Carle wants that'."[107] Jean Carle was Chretien's Director of Operations. Carle would later admit to shredding APEC-related documents[108] and making suggestions to the RCMP about security details to protect Suharto from undergoing any embarrassing criticism of his human rights record.[109]

If the government did nothing wrong, why did they try to interfere with the public inquiry into the APEC affair? Why did the PMO launch an attack against CBC reporter Terry Milewski, who had covered the events?

Every step of the way, the federal government impeded the work of the tribunal, including refusing to co-operate, failing to fund legal counsel for witnesses, impugning the impartiality of its panelists and possibly signaling to the RCMP Public Complaints Commission to shut down or block the proceedings of the tribunal.

As the panel began to collect evidence, Chretien himself said he would not co-operate with the investigation. In January 2000, the federal government argued that the Commission had no jurisdiction over the Prime Minister and that therefore Chretien could not be called to testify. On February 25, the tribunal ruling accepted the argument that it could not compel the Prime Minister's co-operation but requested that Chretien appear as a witness. Needless to say, Chretien did not. His public defence of himself was limited to, "I did not talk to the police myself."[v.] But what about the PMO? It would later become clear that they were in communication with the RCMP during the security planning.

The RCMP Public Complaints Commission chair, Shirley Heafy, is appointed by the government and thus has a vested interest in the outcome of the tribunal findings. Throughout, she obstructed several efforts that would have allowed the tribunal to conduct its investigation properly, including refusing in September 1998 to pay for the legal representation of students who should have been allowed to appear before the tribunal. Eventually the Federal Court of Canada ruled that funding should be provided for the students to retain counsel. Heafy would later admit that she "was under a lot of pressure in Ottawa," although she did not elaborate what kind of pressure this was or where it came from. It appeared to come from the office of the Solicitor General or perhaps Andy Scott himself.[110] Panel chair Gerald M. Morin said after learning about this that he "felt that the independence of the panel was being threatened."[111] He would later resign.

Nearly two months before his December 4 resignation, as the tribunal was just beginning, an NDP Member of Parliament with an impeccable reputation for honesty made public a conversation between Solicitor General Andy Scott and another passenger on an airplane. Dick Proctor took notes of the conversation and later reported that Scott said he was acting as Chretien's cover and the tribunal would find that several RCMP officers overreacted. And the conversation left every impression that the tribunal would make these findings even though the evidence did not necessarily point that way.

Scott said that RCMP Sgt. Hugh Stewart, the officer captured on videotape dousing the protestors in pepper spray, "may be the guy who

---

v. At least one witness, however, said that she saw Chretien order police to ensure that the visiting leaders did not see signs. Lawrence Martin, *Iron Man: The Defiant Reign of Jean Chretien*, p. 200.

takes the fall for this." Later, Scott would deny ever hearing of Stewart, although Fred Toole, the other participant in the now famous conversation, confirmed Proctor's account of the story. Scott was forced to resign on November 23, 1998, more than a month after the conversation took place, and was replaced by Lawrence MacAulay. But it took a month because, once again, the Prime Minister stubbornly resisted opposition demands for the head of one of his cabinet ministers. Lawrence Martin's description of Chretien's reaction to such demands could be the motto of his time in office:"Don't cave to critics. Beat them down. Fight your way through it."[112]

Clearly, the RCMP and the government tried to impede the tribunal. The taint of interference led the entire first panel to resign from the RCMP Public Complaints Commission-appointed tribunal. The second inquiry was a panel of one, presided over by E.N. (Ted) Hughes.

It was not enough for Chretien's government to prevent a full inquiry; it had to prevent any investigation into what Peppergate (as it was beginning to be labeled) was really all about. That also meant there would be an effort to quash any journalistic inquiry.

Without citing specific evidence, Chretien's Director of Communications, Peter Donolo, wrote to the CBC, alleging reporter Terry Milewski was biased against the prime minister. Milewski would no longer cover the APEC affair despite the fact that a CBC ombudsman did not find any evidence of Milewski's bias or any other wrongdoing. Although legislation guarantees the CBC's independence from government intervention, Milewski was never re-assigned to cover APEC. As CBC ombudsman Marcel Pepin noted, "a complaint from the Communications Department of the head of government … takes on unusual importance for the public and all media."[113] Although he said this as an acknowledgment that the letter could be seen as "an indirect threat to the independence of the CBC," his concerns about journalistic independence were not heeded by CBC brass. Again, the PMO had questioned the impartiality of a critic to effectively silence him, just as it had with Gerald Morin.

It is often said that the cover-up is worse than the crime. But if the PMO had any direct or indirect role in leading the RCMP to its use of pepper spray to punish (not merely restrain) protestors, then "Canada's most senior political figures deliberately set in motion a chain of events that ended in the violation of the fundamental rights of large numbers of Canadians."[114] In other words, the freedoms of speech and association and freedom from arbitrary arrest guaranteed by the Charter of Rights and Freedoms that Chretien so proudly admits to having helped craft, meant little when such rights conflicted with Chretien's hold on power.

Some Chretien critics[115] go too far when they say that the APEC affair makes Canada look like a police state, but as Pue noted, "Shielding police from politicians is the foundation of the rule of law."[116] It could also be noted that it is also a foundation of democracy that inquiries into the actions of government should be shielded from political interference. As Jim McNulty wrote in the *Vancouver Province*, "The real problem here is that Canada has no formal mechanism for dealing with the central accusation in this case – political interference in policing by the prime minister and/or his office."[117]

Pue says the APEC affair raises questions about the rule of law and liberty in a democracy and thus the book he edited "is a book about civics."[118] If Peppergate was a civics lesson, the Chretien Liberals failed.

Of course, the final report of the tribunal said no such thing. Ted Hughes found the RCMP acted improperly and that its oppressive actions were the result of poor planning. It also called for changes to the way future inquiries were conducted including asking that the

Public Complaints Commission stay out of them. But, as was noted at the time, the APEC affair was not about police and protests, "It is about Mr. Chretien's government and the extraordinary efforts taken to shield the Prime Minister from attack. Those efforts knew few bounds."[119] Hughes' report was virtually silent on the role of the PMO. One of the protestors, Alissa Westergard-Thorpe, told the UBC student paper, the report misses the "fundamental issue" which was "not the techniques the police used and the administrative details of how they cracked down on protestors, but why they did it, and what it means for a democratic society when that's going on."[120] Hughes, however, ignored these issues.

Not that the formal report mattered. As *Kamloops Daily News* columnist David Charbonneau noted, "Canadians had decided long ago that the Government of Canada was involved in the suppression of demonstrators' constitutional rights."[121] The public may have thought that, but did it matter? Not to Chretien; he carried on as if nothing happened. By the 2000 federal election, APEC was a distant memory.

Why did Chretien treat the APEC inquiry the way he did? The answer can be summed up in just two words: Somalia inquiry. Pue said, "Chretien's government gained experience in first muting and then shutting down an embarrassing inquiry when the Somalia Inquiry moved from considering problems of military governance under the previous Conservative government to looking into apparently unseemly events that took place on the Liberal watch."[122] Chretien and his cronies in the PMO know that obstruction and bullying tactics had worked before, so why not try them again?

A better question is why the public let Chretien get away with this. Part of the answer is that the real issues (the separation of police power and political decision-making; the rule of law; respect for individual liberty and the constitution) are beyond what journalists care to explain to the public. Reporters have difficulty with complex legal issues and weighty philosophical concepts and assume the people who depend upon them for news share their ignorance and impatience. But there were several other issues that muddied the waters on APEC. First, the government successfully portrayed all demonstrators as violent. Indeed, some anti-APEC protestors did rip down a security fence. The subtle distinctions between violent activists and peaceful demonstrators were lost, and in hindsight, the actions of the police were made to seem justifiable. Consequently, there was little public sympathy for what were perceived to be radical student activists who were thought to be at the forefront of organizing the demonstrations. The RCMP and federal government successfully exploited these prejudices. Considering that most of the hearings took place after the violent clashes between anti-globalization protestors and police in Seattle in 1999 (and subsequent confrontations elsewhere), it was easy for the government to claim that security had been the pre-eminent concern at APEC. Lastly, Chretien knew that Canadians cared little for scandal-driven politics, a fact that generally gave him a free pass. As Pue argued, Chretien benefited from it being the least sexy of the continental scandals happening at the time. South of the border, Bill Clinton was embroiled in the indignity of the Monica Lewinsky affair. Chretien, said Pue, "hid behind Mr. Clinton's problems" by suggesting, "we shouldn't be as silly as the Americans" in worrying about issues that have no bearing on the lives of Canadians. This "it's-the-American-way, not-the-Canadian-way" appeal had "intrinsic appeal north of the 49th parallel" and "was a good political strategy."[123]Chretien was lucky that his virulent anti-Americanism was easily sold to the Canadian public at large.

* * * * * *

But long before the report on the APEC affair was released, the country's attention had turned to another scandal. In late 1999, the Liberal Party was about to face the most serious challenge to its credibility. There had already been questions about grants by the Human Resources Development Canada and other agencies to businesses in Jean Chretien's home constituency. However, the HRDC scandal was about to explode. On November 17, Jane Stewart, the newly installed minister responsible for Human Resources Development Canada, saw the results of an audit on how the HRDC doled out grants to 459 randomly selected projects. It revealed a pattern of gross mismanagement, with four-fifths of the projects examined showing "no evidence of financial monitoring." An entire book could be written on the Human Resources Development Canada imbroglio. There are many facets of this scandal including the discovery of $1 billion in reimbursements that had shoddy or non-existent paperwork, or were improperly paid to non-qualifying recipients or dispersed to people with connections to the Prime Minister, cabinet members or the Liberal Party.

The internal audit found that 15 per cent of the projects which received "grants and contributions" did not have an application on file from the sponsor; 72 per cent had no cash flow forecast; 11 per cent had no budget proposal; 11 per cent had no description of expected results; and 87 per cent had no evidence of supervision. Fully 37 per cent of files contained evidence of mismanagement so egregious that a second HRDC investigation was called to determine whether or not the government's cavalier lack of oversight of the dollars spent might actually have risen to the level of criminality, and whether the police should be called in to investigate.[124] At the very least, this was gross mismanagement. To the government's critics, it was possible evidence that the Liberals cut corners in an effort to circumvent the rules in order to pay friends and buy voters. When the internal audit finally became public, the government's critics called the HRDC mess "a billion dollar boondoggle" – and that was based on a random sampling from the $13 billion HRDC budget. In other words, the $1 billion boondoggle was probably just the tip of the iceberg.

The mess became public two months after Stewart first became aware it herself. On January 17, 2000, the Reform Party researcher Laurie Throness[125] made an Access to Information request to see the audit. On January 18, Stewart made the findings of the audit public in a press conference and released the audit the next day. She would later claim the Reform Party's request to see a copy of it had no bearing on the timing of the release of the information. Stewart said she did not even know about the request until January 21. This seems unlikely; as Lawrence Martin has since discovered, "a strange letter from Stewart's office came to light," which purported to show that Stewart and her staff did not have knowledge of the Access to Information request until January 21. However, the letter was dated January 20. Stewart's office conveniently blamed a clerical error. "A secretary forgot to change the date in the computer template that she used to prepare correspondence," wrote Lawrence Martin. "A mere tempest in a template, they said."[126] Considering the previous seven years of lies, obstructions and blame-shifting, the public might be forgiven for being skeptical. How many would believe Stewart's claim that she "hit the roof" when she saw the audit? Walter Robinson, federal director of the Canadian Taxpayer's Federation wondered in a column, "If she was so upset, why did HRDC continue to spend millions?" Indeed, Robinson noted she was so upset about the apparent mismanagement that within the 24 hours after reading the audit, "the Minister signed off on six more HRDC job grant projects totaling close to $1 million."[127]

But, as was the pattern, when something went wrong, the Chretien Liberals continued with business as usual. And, as always, Chretien refused to deal with the problem forthrightly. In his memoirs, former Reform Party leader Preston Manning described the Chretien method of dealing with scandal: "denial mode, to justification mode, to obstruction and [then to] cover-up mode."[128]

The government's reaction to the breaking scandal was predictable. First, the Prime Minister and his HRDC minister denied there was a problem. Later, they would trivialize it. Chretien told the House of Commons, that auditors "found only two problems in seven files" and that these "problems" constituted an "overpayment of $251.50." He had to know that he was highlighting only one, narrow aspect of the audit and that the audit itself was not a comprehensive, but rather a random review of the HRDC spending.

Chretien also defended the lack of accountability by calling it an administrative problem: "Administrative problems of this sort always exist." But no one was ever held accountable to the administrative problems. It's almost as if the government believed they occurred naturally and without human input.

The most common defence was to dismiss concerns about the misspent funds and defend the purpose of the program itself; that is, to justify the expenditures and refuse to answer questions about the lack of oversight for the spending. Indeed, few people questioned the wisdom of the spending, but rather how the grants were administered and the evident potential for abuse because of the lack of oversight.

Chretien said that the Transitional Jobs Fund, an HRDC program where most of the oversight irregularities occurred, provided employment opportunities where none would otherwise exist. He maintained that in any organization the size of the HRDC, mistakes would be made. Anyway, he said, whatever mismanagement there was, their hearts were in the right place because the TJF created jobs and alleviated poverty.

In March 2000, Canadian Alliance MP Grant Hill questioned a $6 million grant given to Bas Iris, a company owned by an individual who gave $21,000 to the Liberal Party just prior to the 1997 election in a Quebec riding (Anjou-Riviere-des-Praires) that was quite closely contested. Stewart's reply was that 1,440 jobs were created. It is noteworthy that Auditor General Denis Desautels said in his October 2000 report, that Stewart's department was generally very lax in following up on whether funding contributed to new jobs and the criteria they did use was faulty. He noted the "HRDC counted all the jobs created by a project, regardless of the extent of its contribution toward the project's total cost."[129] He added that when more than one government program funded projects, they often both claim the total number of new jobs, thereby exaggerating the true role of the government in job creation.

In an example of extraordinary chutzpah, Chretien went on the offensive to deal with persistent questions about the HRDC mess. As opposition members challenged the government on HRDC grants to the Prime Minister's riding during Question Period in the House of Commons, Government House Leader Dan Boudria would hand Chretien sheets of paper from a large, black binder. Chretien would respond by noting how much money went to the opposition member's riding. When Reform MP Deborah Grey asked Boudria for a copy of the information he was providing the Prime Minister so that the party could check the proportion of grants that went to Liberal MP's ridings, she was informed the government did not have riding-by-riding breakdowns of the spending. After initial obstruction, the government was caught in its obvious lies and provided the information to the Opposition.[130]

For the ten months following the revelations of the internal HRDC audit, the opposition regularly called for the resignation of Jane Stewart, and throughout the year 2000 Chretien and Stewart offered a litany of excuses. At one point, the government went so far as to blame its own spending cuts for the problematic lack of paperwork at HRDC saying that the reduced civil service resulted in less oversight and hurried work.[131] According to this defence, the lack of documentation, background checks and follow-up and the application errors were because there just weren't enough workers to oversee the program. The opposition found the real problem to be not enough ministerial responsibility and oversight.

Chretien steadfastly defended his HRDC minister while simultaneously insisting that all his ministers would and should take responsibility for what happened on their watch. It never happened. No cabinet minister resigned during Chretien's decade in power for any direct mistake he or she made *as a cabinet minister*. Jane Stewart "took responsibility" by denying there was a problem, getting re-elected and staying in cabinet. The fact that she and the Liberals were re-elected was read as a sign that voters did not care about the scandals.

Between January and October 2000, the leading critic of the government's HRDC file was Canadian Alliance MP Diane Ablonczy. Her major concern was the spending at the Transitional Jobs Fund, and Ablonczy and her colleagues in the Canadian Alliance would often return to the nagging and unanswered questions about several grants to businesses in Chretien's own riding of Saint-Maurice. Preston Manning said there was "mounting evidence that funds were being systemically allocated to projects for the political benefit of the Liberal Party and its members."[132] The Canadian Taxpayers Federation federal director Walter Robinson noted a disproportionate amount of the TJF program funding spent "in the run-up to or during the 1997 election." And while Liberals would point to opposition ridings that received TJF grants, Robinson noted "these are mostly swing ridings where the Liberals were in tough fights to make gains."[133]

The TJF was rife with problems. Technically, the Transitional Jobs Fund was supposed to give grants to projects in areas with unemployment rates above 12 per cent. But Ablonczy highlighted many projects that did not qualify. For example, Duchess Foods received $2 million to move from low-unemployment Hamilton to the low-unemployment riding of Brant represented by the HRDC minister herself, Jane Stewart.[134] The ridings are practically neighbours. Nor did it make sense to move a company from one low-unemployment riding to another. But Hamilton is more reliably Liberal than rural Brant County. Also, RMH received $1.6 million to relocate to Brant County, even though the company subsequently admitted it would have moved there even without government assistance.

Not only was the TJF supposed to help companies in economically depressed areas, it was supposed to assist small and medium-sized firms. But on at least two occasions, international department store giant Wal-Mart got grants: once, to open a store in Cornwall, one of the few contested Ontario ridings, and the other in Brantford, where a Wal-Mart was built on the outskirts of the city and nearly adjacent to the home riding of Jane Stewart.

Cynics could reasonably view the TJF as a slush fund for the Chretien Liberals; after all, the party was clearly using it as such.

The Reform Party/Canadian Alliance – and to a lesser extent, the Tories – found the HRDC scandal rich in opportunities to criticize the Liberals. They hit them on the abuse of taxpayer money, a possible cover-up by Stewart of the departmental audit, her failure to address continuing concerns about the TJF program (which in 1999 became the Canada Jobs Fund), and a possible connection to Shawinigate. The problem, it seemed, was that there were too many issues and the public became confused. How much easier it would be to hammer away at a case that could be instinctively understood such as the sinfulness of cheating on a spouse with an intern. Republicans had tabloid material for fodder against the Democratic president; Canadian conservatives had accountant ledger sheets where "i"s were un-dotted and "t"s uncrossed.

To the opposition the most damning possibility and the easiest case to make was that some of the projects in the HRDC audit (and other grants, loans and favours found through Access to Information searches by the Canadian Alliance and Progressive Conservative parties and the *National Post*) benefited friends and a client of Chretien in his home riding.

Chretien owned a 25 per cent stake in a golf course near his hometown, Shawinigan, which he sold to Toronto businessman Jonas Prince for $300,000 when he became prime minister. But Prince could not pay the $300,000 and Chretien did not receive a dime until 1999. In the meantime, it appears that Chretien lent an unusual level of support to Yvon Duhaine, a businessman who owned the Auberge Grand-Mere hotel on a property adjacent to the golf course. As members of the opposition noted, by helping the hotel Chretien enhanced the value of the golf course and therefore increased the likelihood that he would be paid back. Chretien claimed to have believed he had already been paid for the property. (When Prince finally did pay Chretien, it was for just more than $200,000 and did not include interest on the six-year-old deal.)

During the 2000 election, the *National Post* reported that Chretien personally lobbied the president of the Business Development Bank, Francois Beaudoin, for a $615,000 loan to Duhaime. Instead of denying the report, Chretien dismissed its significance by justifying the phone calls and meeting: "You know, you call who you know and I know the president, so I called him once or twice. He came to visit me at my home … Fine, it is the normal operation." He later amended his story to include the fact that he considered the BDB to be dragging its feet on a decision about the loan. "I called them, and said, 'Make up your mind'." Lawrence Martin said, "It was quite a blunt order coming from a prime minister, and the fact that he was showing such keen interest in a comparatively small file about the financial arrangements of a loan to a small hotel was bound to arouse suspicion."[135]

Chretien claimed that he was just doing his duty as an MP, the same defence he made for Michel Dupuy in 1995 when the then Heritage Minister contacted the CRTC on behalf of a local radio station. (At least there was a consistency.) But the rules governing such contacts with Crown corporations and federal agencies were changed after the Dupuy affair and, in 1997 David Collenette resigned as Defence Minister because he contacted an immigration tribunal on behalf of a constituent.

The conflict of interest in Shawinigate, however, was greater than when Dupuy or Collenette acted on behalf of their constituents. After all, Chretien had a previous business relationship with Duhaime, who paid Chretien and his partners $200,000 for their stake in the Auberge Grand-Mere.

During the election Chretien referred the case to his ethics counselor, Howard Wilson. Wilson ruled that there was nothing that prevented an MP from communicating with the heads of Crown corporations, including the Prime Minister. Wilson never considered the issues raised by the opposition, namely the apparent conflict of interest. Wilson only ruled – and exonerated Chretien – on the single question that the Prime Minister posed: had he broken any rules or regulations?

Jeffrey Simpson wrote in *The Friendly Dictatorship*, that "no one could prove" Wilson "deliberately doctored reports to exonerate the man who appointed him, but the reporting path from counselor to prime minister suggested to critics that Wilson had at the very least chosen to interpret the evidence in a way favourable to the prime minister." For, as Simpson said, "Wilson would no longer have held his job had he differed publicly with the prime minister's interpretation of events."[136]

Later, the Business Development Bank attempted to sue Duhaime for the delinquent loan. Beaudoin was fired, and in court documents said his removal as head of the Bank was a result of political interference.

It was also revealed that the hotel received money through the Immigrant Investor Program. It was far from clear what role immigrant investors played in the Auberge Grand-Mere but the story kept the infamous hotel and its long list of controversies in the public eye.

Chretien's help was not limited to securing loans. The HRDC's Transitional Jobs Fund also contributed money to Duhaine's hotel. A memo from an aide at HRDC was discovered which said, "we have no choice" but to approve money for the hotel in Chretien's riding despite the fact that it did not qualify for funding.[137] The PMO also directly requested $200,000 from the Canada Economic Development for Quebec Regions for a fountain in the Saint Maurice River in Chretien's riding. The request came from the PMO several weeks *before* the group sponsoring the project applied for funding. When Desautels was asked in a press conference following the release of his report whether there was political interference in the decisions of who was to receive HRDC grants, he said, "We identified a certain number of situations in which standard procedures were not followed."[138]

If there wasn't the appearance of a conflict of interest, the projects had, at the very least, unusual circumstances around them. Reform Party strategist Rick Anderson found it too much of a coincidence that so many projects lacked the proper scrutiny – whether because of the department's institutional lack of checks and balances or mere malfeasance. "There's too much of a pattern here for all this to be random ineptitude," Anderson observed.[139]

After his retirement from politics, Brian Tobin, Chretien's former Fisheries and later Industry minister, zealously (and strangely) defended Chretien against criticism of his apparent conflicts of interest. "I have never seen any evidence that he has one molecule of personal corruption in his body or in his psyche."[140] Perhaps Chretien really did believe that the political interference with the Development Bank, the treating of the TJF as a slush fund for his Liberal Party and the lack of oversight at the HRDC were all justified. But if he did believe that, it was the result of being in power too long; the common good became indistinguishable from his personal interests and he acted accordingly. His brazen defence of the very kind of conduct for which he had earlier lambasted Brian Mulroney was becoming gallingly hypocritical. To be fair to Stewart, the money wasn't spent on her watch but during the time of her predecessors: Alfonse Gagliano, a close friend of Chretien's[141] and Pierre Pettigrew, who was brought into cabinet to shore up support in Quebec in the wake of the narrow federalist win in the 1995 referendum. (In 2004, when Paul Martin became prime minister, the nation became focused on Gagliano once again.) For the time being, Chretien's answer to the Gagliano problem – and probably because he knew what the country wouldn't discover with the advent of Adscam – was to make the former Minister of Public Works, as HRDC was called then, an ambassador. Yes, the punishment for what Gagliano euphemistically referred to as "questionable grants," was to banish him to a comfortable consulate in Europe.

Another central figure in the Public Works/HRDC misspending scandal met a similar fate. Mel Cappe, another friend of Chretien's, was the deputy minister at Human Resources during Gagliano's time there. He would later become clerk of the Privy Council and eventually Canadian High Commissioner to the United Kingdom.

Perhaps Chretien truly believed he was doing the right thing, but it looks suspiciously like he sent two of the central figures from the HRDC scandal off to plum overseas appointments as the controversy was growing.

Considering that many if not most people get much of their news from reading nothing more than the headlines (combined with the sound-bite politics of television), it is surprising that more Canadians were not upset with the scandal. A June 22, 2000 press release by the Canadian Taxpayer's Federation noted headlines that appeared in the previous five months that summarized the corruption: "This isn't sloppiness – it's gross negligence," *Toronto Star* (January 21, 2000); "Current scandal just tip of iceberg," *Ottawa Citizen* (February 3, 2000); "Line between patronage and government grants is fuzzy at best," Canadian Press (February 10, 2000); "Jobs fund dry up after Liberal riding goes NDP," *Globe and Mail* (February 16, 2000); "Job grants 'too political', '97 audit found," *Ottawa Citizen* (February 18, 2000); "Liberals lack any remorse," *Windsor Star* (February 18, 2000); "Stewart accused of cover-up in report of HRDC payments," *Globe and Mail* (February 23, 2000); "Firms spent job grants but produced nothing," *Hamilton Spectator* (March 3, 2000); "HRDC scandal: Worst yet to come," *Ottawa Citizen* (March 8, 2000); "Welcome to Grantford," *Brantford Expositor* (March 10, 2000); "PM's riding got more cash than Alberta," *National Post* (March 16, 2000). Why did the Chretien Liberals get away with the HRDC scandal? *Edmonton Sun* columnist Paul Stanway said Chretien did what he always did: "deny, excuse, confuse" and "sooner or later, the attention of the notoriously fickle Canadian media and electorate will wane … and the crisis will pass."[142] He made these observations just two weeks after the scandal first came to light and ten months before the federal election.

True to form, Chretien denied there was a problem, excused it as a worthwhile way to create jobs and confused the issue, drawing in facts that had little to do with the actual controversy. In the end, he simply denied there was any need to take responsibility for any of it. But the HRDC misspending fiasco was complicated, and when voters could not easily figure out what had happened, they ignored the issue. Lawrence Martin said, "Voters had, quite understandably, chosen not to wade into the thicket of detail on the complex story and were still prepared to give Chretien the benefit of the doubt, especially when they had no one else to turn to."[143] Often, it seemed, the only people who cared about how HRDC spent $1 billion without proper documentation, were the opposition parties and the press gallery.

In February 2000, Stanway began his column by asking, "Does the Shovelgate fiasco really have the potential to damage the Chretien government's re-election chances? Only if the previous paragraph needed no explanation to the majority of Canadian voters." By October, even though the Auditor General released a damning report on HRDC's misuse of taxpayers' money just days before the federal election call, the public had tuned out. Canadians simply didn't understand the intricacies of the issue, and they no longer cared.

When the facts started to show that Chretien might have been personally tied to some of the loans, and actually stood to benefit from some of them, the Opposition thought it had found an angle that could be understood by the public; an issue on which it could score some political points. But even Shawinigate did not jolt voters into understanding the scandalous nature of the Chretien Liberals. And the affair would also have a connection to what could be argued was Chretien's most self-servingly arrogant act, the significance of which was never fully appreciated by the Canadian public.

* * * * * *

In 1999, then-British Conservative Party leader William Hague nominated newspaper baron Conrad Black for a peerage. Prime Minister Tony Blair accepted and proposed that the Queen name Black to the House of Lords. In accordance with customary practices, the

British government informed the Canadian High Commission in London who responded in writing that Black could receive the honour once he obtained dual citizenship and did not use his title in Canada. Black was set to be appointed a Lord on June 17, 1999 but two days before the pronouncement, Chretien nixed the appointment citing an obscure and rarely invoked 1919 Parliamentary resolution. Chretien's move, the *National Post* editorialized, was "a gesture calculated to embarrass Mr. Black."[144]

The Nickle resolution, passed 80 years earlier, promulgated that Canadian citizens *should* not receive foreign honours; specifically, it requested that King George V refrain from granting titles to Canadians. It should be remembered that the Nickle Resolution was passed in the aftermath of World War I, when nationalism and suspicion of foreign governments was high. And, as the *Post* said, it was "never binding, legally obsolete and inapplicable as it referred to Canadian citizens and residents." In contrast, Chretien had no concerns that Bill Graham, the Toronto MP whom the Prime Minister eventually appointed the Minister of Foreign Affairs, received the Chevalier of the Legion of Honour from France. And as the *Daily Telegraph*[5] reported, "Constitutional experts argued that the resolution had no statutory force. The resolution had largely been ignored over the past 80 years, during which 20 knighthoods and two peerages have been granted to Canadians."[145] In 1988, Prime Minister Brian Mulroney reaffirmed the Nickle Resolution but in doing so acknowledged that foreign honours could be bestowed to Canadians with dual citizenship. The Nickle Resolution clearly did not have, as the Chretien Privy Council claimed, statutory force. It was, after all, a resolution, not legislation. As the *Daily Telegraph* reported in June 1999, "in a 1933 debate of the Canadian House of Commons the then prime minister, Richard Bennett, said that the Nickle Resolution did not limit the sovereign's exercise of rights, which could be done only by statute."[146]

Chretien claimed he was only following Canadian tradition, ignoring the 20 knighthoods and two peerages as well as the French government distinction given to a member of his own cabinet. To give himself some cover, Chretien appointed his Deputy Prime Minister, Herb Gray, to look at the issue. He would ultimately find that Chretien acted in accordance with the Nickle Resolution and tradition, but as Lawrence Martin reported even Gray's wife, Sharon Scholzberg-Gray, president of the Canadian Healthcare Association, thought her husband's examination of the peerage denial was farcical. "The Prime Minister," she said, "had made the decision before the committee studied it."[147]

Whatever the technicalities, Chretien asked the Queen to deny the peerage, knowing full well that she would not refuse his request; she would not want to create an international incident by ignoring the plea of the Canadian prime minister.

In his request to the Queen, he tellingly noted that one of Black's paper's, the *National Post*, had investigated alleged improprieties of businesses with ties to the prime minister. (Black would later note that the Prime Minister complained about this to him personally. Chretien biographer Lawrence Martin said that the Prime Minister would "phone Black every now and then to register his discontent."[148]) Chretien appeared to admit that he was opposing Black's peerage out of revenge. The Prime Minister was using his office to satisfy a personal sense of pique.

Black sued the prime minister arguing, plausibly, that Chretien had abused his power as part of a vendetta that arose from Black's newspaper empire's coverage of the endless Liberal scandals. Despite having a cordial relationship with Chretien that went back 20 years,[149] Black was a vociferous critic of the Liberal government. He had appointed numerous editors who shared his broadly conservative ideological leanings to key posts at several newspapers, most notably Kenneth Whyte at the helm of the *National Post*, Peter Stockland as the editor of the *Montreal Gazette* and, in 1998, William Watson and John Robson as the editorial page editor and deputy editorial page editor respectively, at the rejuvenated *Ottawa Citizen*.

The Ontario Court of Appeal dismissed Black's suit in May 2001, claiming the Prime Minister's "prerogative power relating to the granting of honours" is beyond judicial review. The three-member court panel said that, "even if the advice was wrong or careless or negligent, even if his motives were questionable, they cannot be challenged by judicial review." The ruling did not directly address the legal issues Black's complaint had raised, nor did it acknowledge that Black was also a British citizen. Black subsequently renounced his Canadian citizenship and, on September 11, 2001 became Lord Black of Crossharbour.

While most of the major media ignored the implications of the feud, the *Post* editorialized that Chretien had clearly "used the discretionary powers of his office to harass a prominent Canadian media owner for the simple reason that he felt threatened and affronted by this newspaper's legitimate investigations" and "that he abused Mr. Black's status as a dual citizen to meddle in and diminish his civil rights as a citizen of the United Kingdom."[150] The paper rightly noted that had it been anyone else, "there would be a howl of righteous outrage from the press over a case of attempted state censorship." But the media ignored the real issues and Chretien got away with using his office to further a personal vendetta; because he didn't like the press coverage in the newspapers Black owned, he attempted to deny Black his peerage.

Several months after Black renounced his Canadian citizenship, he sold his 20 per cent share of the *National Post* and his other Canadian newspaper holdings, the Southam chain that included newspapers in

Montreal, Ottawa, Calgary, Edmonton and Vancouver. Chretien had manoeuvred one of his most outspoken critics out of the newspaper business in Canada. Black sold the papers to CanWest Global Communications, which had already co-owned the *National Post*.

Chretien's self-serving and vindictive denial of Black's peerage would be one thing if it were just another venal stunt. But as a *National Post* editorial said after Black took his seat in the House of Lords, while Lord Black of Crossharbour "richly deserves the honour ... bestowed in recognition of his contributions to British public life," he "deserves honour even more here than in Britain.[151] A winner of the Order of Canada in 1990, Black was a successful entrepreneur, "a man of diverse achievements," the Governor General called him, and a generous supporter of Canadian charities. The country had lost one of the last few real believers in print journalism, not just in Canada, but the world. He bled money building the *National Post*, a paper that made the whole industry better. As the *Post* noted, and many observers of the state of Canadian journalism agree, Black "did more than anyone to enliven Canadian newspapers – most notably by founding the *National Post*," which forced other papers to improve their layout and breadth of coverage.

Furthermore, the *Post* "shatter[ed] the stultifyingly narrow confines of this country's political debate."[152] That, however, was precisely the problem; Black and his papers challenged the status quo, including the completely unquestioning acceptance by the mainstream media of the soft socialism of the country's so-called social programs. Furthermore, the *Post*'s and the improved *Ottawa Citizen*'s focus on Ottawa forced all the papers to beef up their Parliamentary bureaus. With more reporters crawling over Ottawa, there were more Access to Information searches, more tracking down of rumours of misconduct. None of this served Chretien's goal of governing without scrutiny. With the advent of the *National Post*, all papers were scrutinizing the federal government a little more closely. Chretien had to punish Black and the only way he could achieve that was to deny him the peerage. As Lawrence Martin said of the peerage denial, it was "a new application of the Shawinigan chokehold he once put on a protestor."[153]

It is unclear if Chretien knew that Black would ultimately leave over the petty prevention of the peerage. It was enough, for Chretien, to merely punish the *Post*'s proprietor. But Chretien certainly couldn't have been disappointed with Black's departure.

That self-serving arrogance would force from this country one of the few "leaders urging us to make the most of ourselves and play a significant role in world affairs ... But for the smallness of a handful of men in Ottawa, the contributions he will continue to make to the richness of public life in the United Kingdom could have been shared with Canada."[154]

When the Ontario Court of Appeals decision was announced, Black said he would have to reconsider his dual citizenship: "For a wide range of reasons, citizenship of Canada is not now for me." He said in a statement released just three hours after the decision was rendered, "Having opposed for 30 years precisely the public policies that have caused scores of thousands of educated and talented Canadians to abandon their country every year, it is at least consistent that I should join this dispersal." Those, of course, were the policies of Jean Chretien and Prime Ministerial predecessors he served under as the finance and justice minister, including Pierre Trudeau and Lester B. Pearson. The whole affair, Mark Steyn would later observe, was "an exquisite embodiment of psychologically crippled small-mindedness."[155]

But Chretien was all small-mindedness. He sought the office of the Prime Minister not to pursue an agenda but to hold power. With that power he directed funds to friends – individuals and companies that had donated to the Liberal Party or its MPs, and candidates that needed pork provided for their constituents and voters. He used his office to settle scores with a newspaper owner whose newspapers had the audacity to actually report the shocking scandals that they uncovered.

This was hardly the legacy with which Chretien would want to leave office. He might have left in 2000 or 2001 had it not been for another feud. This feud was with someone much closer and potentially more dangerous to him than a critical newspaper baron; this feud was with his Finance Minister, Paul Martin. To prevent Martin from getting his job, and to prevent the appearance that he was being pushed out of office, Chretien would call another early election.

CHAPTER FIVE

2000 ELECTION

O n October 15, 2000, the federal government released a so-called "mini–budget", just days before an election call. In it, Paul Martin announced $100 billion in tax cuts over five years and mandated $10 billion to begin paying off the debt, thus adopting the Canadian Alliance's agenda, and even stealing the best issues away from them.[156]

The budget also included a rebate cheque to cover the heating expenses for lower-income Canadians. Many voters were becoming concerned about rising fuel prices and this one-time payout would be a visible demonstration to Canadians that Liberals were paying attention, or perhaps better yet, paying for their attention. The following year, the Auditor General would discover that thousands of cheques went to dead Canadians, the incarcerated and others who simply didn't qualify for the money. In fact, almost 40 per cent of the rebate cheques went to people who should not have received them. The budget also featured an increase in Employment Insurance benefits, a sop to Atlantic Canadian voters (in the form of allowing seasonal workers to collect EI) who had thrown out almost half of the Liberal MPs in the previous election as punishment for EI cuts in the mid 1990s.

Also, Brian Tobin, the popular premier of Newfoundland, returned to cabinet. Tobin, a former Fisheries Minister who gained fame in 1994 fighting against a Portuguese turbot fishery on the fringes of Canadian water, had left the federal cabinet in December 1995 to become premier of Newfoundland. To rebound in Atlantic Canada, Chretien would need big name Liberals such as Tobin and former New Brunswick premier Frank McKenna; days before the October 22 election call, Tobin was installed in cabinet. *The Report* magazine found Chretien's "vaulting" of Tobin "back into cabinet" to be "a breathtaking display of the arbitrary use of power to achieve the prime minister's political and personal goals."[157] In lieu of new ideas, Chretien tried to lure big names to run as Liberal candidates, including such hand-appointed nominees as Royal Bank of Canada chief economist John McCallum and University of Victoria law professor Stephen Owen. Chretien had less success with others; he tried, and failed, to convince Winnipeg mayor Glen Murray and former Saskatchewan NDP Premier Roy Romanow to run for the Liberals.

But Tobin was the prize catch, and he may have made the difference in Atlantic Canada. After years of neglecting the region, his nomination was seen as a signal to Maritimers that their concerns were now Chretien's concerns. Whatever may have happened in the previous seven years, Chretien wanted to show that he now cared about the region, and Tobin was pegged as the goodwill ambassador to get that message across.

It was clear that the Liberals knew this election could be close, and that they could not take Atlantic Canada for granted; indeed, they were looking to actively win back some seats in the Maritimes that had been lost in the previous election. Gains in this region and in Quebec would offset any potential losses in Ontario if their smear campaign against Stockwell Day did not work in Central Canada.

A month before the mini-budget, Chretien announced a new Health Accord with the provinces, a deal that increased federal transfer payments by nearly 40 per cent over five years. In anticipation of the election, the Liberals let the spigots flow and opened the federal vault. Throughout his first seven years as prime minister, Jean Chretien rebuffed opposition concerns about Canada's high taxes saying he would not buy the votes of Canadians with tax cuts.

But that was then and this was the eve of an election. The rules changed because it was to the Chretien Liberals' advantage that the rules changed; taxpayers would get a small break and the floodgates of federal spending would be opened. Taxpayers were to be bought with their own money. The most notable thing in the mini-budget was a complete about face on a series of reforms to employment insurance that had been made in the previous seven years. Michael Bliss said, "In the 2000 election campaign, the Liberals reached a new low level in political cynicism by casually bribing a whole region of the country in restoring wildly generous unemployment benefits for seasonal workers."[158]

The election was called within weeks of the September by-elections that had put Stockwell Day and Joe Clark into the Commons. In early October, polls showed the Canadian Alliance closing the gap with the Liberals, most notably in Ontario where they had risen to 25 per cent support. Stockwell Day, the new CA leader, was young and telegenic, garnering some early comparisons to Pierre Trudeau. More importantly, the Chretien Liberals thought Day might have been able to capture the imagination of Canadians with his bold ideas, including a single-rate "flat tax" of 17 per cent.

The Liberals soon recognized that the more the public saw of the Opposition Leader, the more they had to lose, and they knew that the opposition was hoping for an early 2001 election.

Chretien exploited the unprepared Alliance. The party was less than a year old, had just fought an exhausting two-round leadership race, gotten its leader into Parliament with a by-election and did not yet have a full slate of candidates. Chretien might also have wondered if the CA's financial supporters would be able to donate to a leadership contest and a federal election in such quick succession. *Toronto Sun* columnist Bob MacDonald said the early election call – a "$200 million dice roll" that "won big" – demonstrated "that Chretien was politically cunning" in thwarting CA efforts to organize.[159]

The now defunct *Report* (and others) called the election Chretien's "vanity campaign."[160] Just three years into his second mandate, Chretien was fighting off potential attacks from two fronts; within the Liberal Party Paul Martin was openly vying to replace him, while at the same time the improving poll numbers for the Canadian Alliance were starting to become a threat from the outside. Added to that was the challenge of becoming the first prime minister since Mackenzie King to "threepeat" – win three elections in a row.

The opposition parties were not ready for an election, but they thought Chretien was vulnerable. The polls indicated otherwise; although the Alliance Party was gaining in popularity, it was still far behind the Liberals. An Ekos Research Associates poll conducted in late September and early October had the Liberals at 50 per cent, and leading the Alliance in Ontario by a remarkable 59 per cent to 15 per cent. In fact, the Liberals were ahead in every province except Alberta. A COMPAS Poll conducted October 10-12 showed a slightly closer but still not very encouraging race for the opposition; the Liberals led the Alliance 45 to 25 per cent nationally, with an even larger lead in

Ontario. The sole source of good polling news for the Alliance was an Ipsos-Reid poll that found support had reached 25 per cent in Ontario by October 1 compared to a mere nine per cent for the Tories.

Chretien looked at the polls and knew it was time to call an election; he had to prevent a possible Alliance surge. But another factor also led him to the early election. On October 1, former Prime Minister Pierre Elliot Trudeau died. Could it be that Chretien hoped to translate the sentimentalism following Trudeau's death into greater Liberal support? The Prime Minister even publicly mused about renaming Yukon's Mount Logan, Mount Trudeau. If the Chretien Liberals had no vision to offer Canada, they could ride to victory on the memory of a deceased prime minister who certainly *did* have a vision for Canada. In his contribution to a volume of essays examining the 2000 election, University of Toronto political scientist Stephen Clarkson wondered whether in calling the "premature contest," Chretien's arrogance would lead to his party's defeat; whether calling an early election for clear partisan advantage would become the defining issue of the campaign.[161] Joe Clark said that Chretien "walked off the job" and cost the taxpayers $200 million for a needless election.

But the Liberals' opponents lacked unity and this problem did not merely afflict the right side of the political spectrum. With four opposition parties, there would never be a coherent criticism of Chretien or his government, either during Question Period, in the House of Commons or during an election campaign. The parties each had a different message and they were all competing with one other to get those messages heard. The Liberals would always get media time for their position, while "equal time" meant that their opponents would have to share the allotment of opposition time four ways. This meant that there was no single voice able to rise above the din to question the timing of the election call.

The Canadian Alliance made the first serious attempt at doing this. In 1999, Preston Manning had hosted the United Alternative Conference in Ottawa, a meeting of Canadian conservatives that tried to bring Reform and Tories under one "big tent" again. In early 2000, Reform transformed itself (some say it merely rebranded itself) into the Canadian Alliance. Despite the fact that many Tories from Mike Harris' Common Sense Revolution got behind the initiative (including Tom Long as a candidate to lead the new party), many federal Tories did not embrace the new "Alliance". And Chretien knew he had to seek his third mandate while there were still divisions on the right.

These divisions accorded the Liberals many advantages beyond vote splitting. Peter G. White and Adam Daifallah wrote in *Gritlock: Are the Liberals in Forever?*, that the divided right allowed the Liberals to paint themselves as moderates, especially compared to the more conservative Canadian Alliance, much more so than they had ever been able to do against the Progressive Conservative Party.[162] To this end, the Liberals slandered Stockwell Day as a religious zealot and a socially conservative extremist to keep voters in the Liberal camp.

Furthermore, White and Daifallah said that disunity on the right produced not just vote splitting but "candidate-splitting, money-splitting, worker-splitting and strategist-splitting."[163] Also, the intramural fighting turned off voters: both opposition parties looked amateurish and not very much like "governments-in-waiting", and the Liberals clearly benefited from that perception. Whether it actually won votes for them or whether it simply kept would-be Alliance voters at home, there's no doubt the bottom line was a boon for Chretien and his party.

On October 22, after surveying the political landscape and determining that the time was ripe for another Liberal victory, Jean Chretien announced the country would go to the polls on

November 27. Stephen Clarkson said the 2000 election call illustrated that Chretien was not only "unchallengeable in power" but "secretive in his exercise of it." Chief Electoral Officer Jean-Pierre Kingsley said Chretien's "snap election call caught Elections Canada off guard ... and prevented the agency from overhauling its national voters list to fix major shortfalls."[164]

Chretien's decision, whether viewed as calculated or capricious, clearly illustrated one thing: the Prime Minister, and he alone, wielded the power in the Liberal Party. Even the Party's Ontario headquarters in Toronto was kept in the dark about the date until just a few weeks before the actual call – a questionable move considering that this was the office that was responsible for coordinating campaigns for most of the seats the Liberals held in Parliament.[165]

The campaign itself was notable for the unprecedented level of negative campaigning by a Liberal team that sought not merely to defeat their opponents but also to completely vilify them and destroy any credibility they might have had. As Paul Bunner noted in the pages of *The Report*, "It was some of the most vicious, personal and utterly fabricated campaign invective ever seen in Canadian politics."[166] It is one thing to criticize an opponent's record and proposed agenda – in fact, it could be argued that candidates are obligated to do that as part of the discourse that is an election campaign. But the Liberals raised the spectre of a hidden agenda on the part of the Alliance, and particularly on the part of Stockwell Day himself. The Liberals did not merely criticize and attack Day; indeed, they demonized him.

They resorted to a tried and true method of destroying the public image of their opponents. Just as Chretien relished the opportunity to get one last shot in on Mulroney during the Airbus affair and mercilessly criticized Preston Manning as a rube as he was both from the West and religious (a double whammy in the Chretien Liberals' view) in the 1997 election campaign, he relentlessly attacked Day for his "scary" and "un-Canadian" values. The strategy was foreshadowed during a meeting of Third Way politicians at the Berlin Conference on Progressive Governance, June 1-3, 2000, when Chretien warned of the "forces of darkness" that were the Canadian Alliance, even before Day had won the new party's leadership. Chretien sought to polarize the public, hoping that a majority of voters would see the Liberal Party as the protector of "Canadian values", or at least of Canadian social programs. Indeed, presenting the competing values of the two parties to the Canadian people was part of the rationale for the early election: "This election offers two very different visions of Canada," declared the Prime Minister. "Two crystal clear alternatives."

Chretien and his campaign team wasted little time in attacking Day for his alleged hidden agendas on abortion and healthcare, claiming he wanted to privatize health care and outlaw abortion. As luck would have it, an Alliance document entitled *The Policy Overview* came to light. Although it was simply a candidate's briefing document – one that all parties provide to their candidates – the media and the Liberals insinuated it was something more sinister. The paper said that a referendum should be called on an issue when three per cent of voters signed a petition. Day's opponents claimed this was designed to force an easy and quick referendum on abortion. The document also briefed candidates on how to answer questions on the sale of the CBC and extending the GST to native reserves. Chretien declared these ideas to be un-Canadian and wondered why they were not given more prominence. The criticism put the Alliance and Day on the defensive, and for the rest of the campaign they were unable to dispel the perception that they were hiding something.

It has been said that the 2000 election "was the Liberal hatchet-men's finest hour."[167] The hatchet-man *par excellence* was Warren Kinsella, a lawyer and bulldog political operative who, more than anyone, vilified

Stockwell Day and made him look ridiculous. Day himself ran a woeful campaign. That he would not campaign on Sundays helped the Chretien Liberals (and their willing accomplices, the media) portray Day as a dangerous fundamentalist. But the *coup de grace* was the CBC airing of a "documentary" on Day's Christianity that ridiculed his religious beliefs, including his views on creationism. The federal Liberals, like most voters in Alberta, knew of Day's social conservatism. In the 1980s he had been the pastor of an evangelical church. As a member of the provincial legislature in the 1990s he opposed the extension of new and special rights to homosexuals, opposed taxpayer funding of abortion and expressed his concern about the content of books that were being taught in public schools. He also believed in creationism. In other words, Day was like millions of other Canadians in the views he held. "Fundamental Day," a CBC documentary by Paul Hunter, covered what was actually quite well known ground to those who were familiar with Day's history, but it provided the Liberals with an opportunity to paint their primary opponent as a radical fundamentalist. As Kinsella wrote in his defence of attack and demolition campaigning, *Kicking Ass in Canadian Politics*, the airing of the documentary was so "important" because it addressed issues and themes that the Liberal Party wanted to address but couldn't.[168] Kinsella knew, as most wily political strategists do, that it is best to let the media lead and then jump into the fray.

Immediately after the documentary aired, Kinsella called Francois Ducros, the prime minister's director of communications, and Cyrus Reporter, chief of staff to then Health Minister Allan Rock. Kinsella, Ducros and Reporter were part of the Liberal Party's election campaign communications team and as Kinsella recalled, Reporter said the CBC program was "what we've been waiting for."[169]

Kinsella said in his book that believing in creationism is politically irrelevant, that Day has a "constitutional right to believe in whatever he desires," and that an individual's "religious views [are] immaterial to his fitness for public office." In theory. In practice, however, if a politician tears down the wall of separation between his own beliefs and what he does in office, there is a problem. (One might wonder: do Chretien, Kinsella and others act on something other than their own beliefs? Why are secular beliefs better than religious ones?) Author David Frum has said that many Liberals have no problem with religion as long as it is meaningless; something one practices for an hour or so on the weekend and ignores the rest of their week. But Kinsella condemned Day and others for attempting "to infect the public agenda with their religious views."[170]

Instead of attempting to understand Day's religious beliefs – and perhaps even engaging in a serious debate about the role of religion in public life, or even how Day's specific views might play out in the public square – Kinsella and his crew thought it was better to mock those views, and by extension, the views of all Canadian Christians who shared Day's positions.

During the election, Kinsella was a regular panelist on CTV. On November 16, with just a little more than a week left in the campaign, the Liberal strategist went to the studio with a gym bag, the contents of which would end the CA campaign and Day's leadership. Near the end of the segment, Kinsella dismissed a direct question and got ready the gym bag that had been seated beside his chair. He had prepared a stunt with Ken Polk and John Milloy of the Liberal election "war room" that would clinch the public perception of the CBC's "Fundamental Day." Kinsella said: "Valerie [Pringle], you say you want to talk about the past week. Let's do that. In the past day or so, we have learned that Stockwell Day apparently believes that the world is 6,000 years old, Adam and Eve were real people and – my personal favourite – humans walked the earth with dinosaurs. Valerie, I want to remind Mr. Day that *The Flintstones* was not a documentary." And, pulling a stuffed purple

Barney dinosaur out of his gym bag said, "And this is the only dinosaur that recently co-existed with humans."

Recalling the incident in his book, Kinsella said, "Of all the things I have done in politics, over many, many years, probably nothing has had the impact of those few seconds on *Canada A.M.*" Not only had Kinsella and his accomplices raised the spectre of Day's religious views "infecting" the public square, they created the perception "that he was a kook."[171] As then *National Post* columnist Paul Wells said, "The transformation of Mr. Day from Stock to Laughingstock, was complete."[172]

Kinsella defended his stunt claiming, "Canadian voters had no desire to elect a prime minister who would attempt to stick his religion in their faces."[173] This, despite the fact Day seldom brought up religion (or abortion or homosexuality, for that matter) except in answer to the incessant questions of reporters.

But scaring voters with Day's supposed extreme social conservatism was not limited to mocking responses on morning shows. In a television ad that appeared only in Alberta and British Columbia, the Liberals said Day opposed funding for the abortions of victims of rape or incest or in cases where the life of the mother was threatened. While this story is often repeated, there is some evidence that it was another Alberta MLA that uttered the words the advertisement put into Day's mouth.

The concern for the truthfulness of the advertisement's claim was secondary to the need to help the party's incumbents in close elections in Vancouver, Victoria and Edmonton. The Liberals also ran an ad in Western urban centres exploiting an impolitic statement by a Manitoba candidate, Betty Granger. In a generally pro-immigrant speech in Winnipeg, Granger thrice used the unfortunate term "Asian invasion." The media dutifully suggested the party had done little to fix the problem that plagued the Alliance's predecessor, the Reform Party, namely MPs and candidates making injudicious remarks about race. The Liberals ran a commercial in Western Canada's urban centres that ensured immigrants would remain reliable Liberal voters.

Elinor Caplan, the Immigration Minister, was herself in a tight race in her heavily Jewish north-of-Toronto riding of Thornhill, and accused the Alliance of being associated with "Holocaust deniers, prominent bigots and racists," even though the party had expelled members such as Paul Fromm and Douglas Christie[vi] who were connected to racist organizations. Hedy Fry, the Vancouver MP and Minister of State for Multiculturalism, said Day's Christianity was "an insult to every Muslim, Buddhist, Sikh – everybody else who believes in other religions."

There was little debate among the parties about the competing visions for the future of Canada because the Liberals dismissed as frightening, extreme and bigoted the views of their only serious competitor, the Canadian Alliance. There is little need to examine competing views if, as the Chretien Liberals did, those views are simply distilled into "we're the good guys" and "they're the bad guys". In that kind of context, there's really not much to discuss. Opponents and their positions, rather than being analyzed for what they truly are, are simply caricatured, derided, and ultimately dismissed as "scary", "dangerous", or downright "evil".

The ruthless attacks on the CA's supposed extremism and Day's personal beliefs, character, and competence began on the first day of the campaign and never really let up, and that clearly knocked the Opposition leader off his game plan. William Christian, a University of Guelph professor of political science, explained that, "Day wanted to

---

vi. Paul Fromm was the founder of Canadians for Foreign Aid Reform and a frequent speaker at Heritage Front events. Douglas Christie is a lawyer whose clients have included holocaust deniers Ernst Zundel and Jim Keegstra.

establish an image for the party. And then Jean Chretien suckered him. In effect, the Alliance changed its strategy."[174] This helps explain the inept campaign[175] of the Canadian Alliance. Throughout the election, despite the smear campaign against him and his party, Stockwell Day maintained his naive "campaign of respect". The Tories, on the other hand, ran sophomoric ads modeled on the old K-Tel record commercials, calling Chretien a liar.

Whereas attacks on Day stuck, the opposition could barely make a dent in the Liberal armour. When dogged by continued questions about his role in a \$625,000 Business Development Corporation loan to a company owned by an individual who may have been indirectly involved in increasing the value of property of which Chretien was once an owner, the Prime Minister played the victim card and lashed out at his opponents: "Mr. Clark and Mr. Day have overstepped the accepted bounds of fairness and decency ... They have sought to destroy my reputation and in doing so have demeaned the political process." He called the criticism signs of Clark and Day's "desperation". The Liberal leader and his minions would attack the party's opponents with impunity, but any questions about the shady business dealings Chretien was involved in immediately made him indignant that someone would dare to impugn his "integrity".

The double standard worked. The Liberals were re-elected to their third term and Chretien became the first Liberal to lead his party to back-to-back majorities since Louis St. Laurent (1948-1957) and the first to lead his party to three consecutive majorities since Mackenzie King did it in 1935, 1940 and 1945. But as in the previous election, the Liberals had actually done very little to capture the imagination of Canadian voters. And their most recent term had been dogged by scandals. Why were they rewarded with a third majority in Parliament?

Elections are decided not by a single event or issue, and there seems to be a constellation of reasons the Chretien Liberals won in 2000. The economy seemed strong. The Liberals sold themselves as the only national party while hammering the Alliance as an extension of the regional 'rump'; the same brush they used to successfully tar Preston Manning's Reform Party in 1997. They also painted the Alliance as a threat to universal health care, and generally as a party of "extreme"[176] positions. The Liberals ran an effective and disciplined campaign, staying "on message" throughout almost all of it (regardless of how untrue or objectionable that message may have been). The Alliance, on the other hand, was not prepared for the election and ran a terrible campaign. Another reason for the win was the inherent regional weaknesses of the Bloc Quebecois, the NDP and the PCs.

The Bloc, obviously, could not realistically hope to form the government. Instead they sought, (as they had always done), to highlight the concerns of one province. While the Liberals fought the separatist party mostly in an attempt to win just enough seats to maintain their majority in Parliament, the Bloc had a solid hold on a single region, a hold that would not grow, but wouldn't shrink very much either.

The slow disintegration of the NDP also helped the Liberals. If the NDP were to disappear (as it did in some regions), the Liberals would naturally absorb most of the party's supporters – at least those that remained politically involved. This process was already under way as the NDP became more socialist in their orientation and turned off many centrist voters. As the right became and remained divided, the centre-left slowly congealed around the Liberals.

Furthermore, the radical left had become divided. Labour unions complained about the lack of radicalism by the NDP while the anti-globalization movement moved from elective politics and political parties to street protests and organizing over the Internet. This led to the formation of small splinter parties and movement in the ideological territory where the NDP had previously held sway – Mel Hurtig's National Party, Paul Hellyer's Canadian Action Party, and the David Orchard faction within the Tories. All siphoned votes from the small and already ineffective NDP. As New Democrats dipped below 10 per cent in the polls the media ignored them, sending the party into a spiral and leaving the Liberals as the water-carriers for the so-called "progressive" politics in Canada. The vast majority of the electorate had dismissed the NDP as a group of ideologically rigid leftists.

Between the 1997 and 2000 elections, some on the political left tried to refashion the party as the Third Way, similar to Tony Blair in England and Bill Clinton's so-called "New Democrats" in the United States. But there was little interest by the activist wing of the party in broadening their appeal by becoming less ideological. More importantly, Chretien himself successfully put into practice the theory of the Third Way, namely that the centre-left accept and work within certain market realities. It is precisely because the Liberals, a formerly centre-left party, borrowed liberally from such Tory, Reform and Alliance policies as free trade, balanced budgets, and paying off the debt, that the government prevented the NDP from becoming a Third Way party.

* * * * * *

Tory leader Joe Clark could hardly be taken seriously. A one-time prime minister who held onto power in a short-lived minority government in 1979, Clark recaptured the Tory leadership in 1998 when no one else wanted it. The gist of his electoral message was that he should be prime minister again because he was not the Liberal or Canadian Alliance party leader. While Chretien had no vision, he could at least claim to be a competent manager. Clark, on the other hand, had no vision and had proven in 1979 that he was anything but a competent manager.

Clark also handicapped himself by appearing to be campaigning for the job of Leader of the Official Opposition.[177] Unfortunately for Clark, Canadians have never really voted for the second place party.

As polls showed the Alliance closing the gap with the Liberals in Ontario, Chretien raised the spectre of a minority government. Canadians, it seems, have a fear of minority or coalition governments. Often, the spectre of unstable Italian or Israeli parliaments is cited; parliaments where governments fall, it is often joked, almost on an annual basis. Chretien exploited this fear by raising the alarm about a possible minority government; Ontarians responded by giving him 100 of their 103 seats.

The Liberal leader must have also sensed that the public was beginning to grow tired, if not irritated, with his long stay at 24 Sussex. During the campaign, Chretien hinted repeatedly that he would step down part way through whatever mandate was given to him. In essence, he seemed to be inviting Canadians to vote not just for him, but also for Paul Martin, his presumed successor in the Liberal leadership. There is ample evidence that many people who voted Liberal did so because they wanted the fiscal policies of the Finance Minister continued and they hoped that some day, Martin would become prime minister. The November 27 vote, it could be said, gave a mandate to both the winning and the future prime ministers. On election night, Liberal MP Albina Guarnieri, the former *Globe and Mail* reporter who now represented Mississauga East, said voters "didn't want to run the risk of having anybody but Paul Martin run their finances."[178] While the Alliance, NDP, and Tories were running against an unpopular prime minister, many Liberals knew that enough voters would hold their noses when it came to Chretien and ultimately consider their vote a vote for Martin.

It is commonplace for conservatives to complain about media bias against them, but the media certainly had a role in Stockwell Day's demise. Although Day had the embarrassing Sea-Doo incident in September 2000 during which the Alliance leader conducted an outdoor press conference in a red wet-suit after making a grand entrance on a motorized water scooter, the prime minister had his own goofy photo-op seven months earlier. To prove that he was not yesterday's man, an old fogey staying in office past his prime, Chretien went downhill skiing, a favourite past-time of his. (Recall Chretien missed the funeral of Jordan's King Hussein in 1999 because he was skiing in Whistler, B.C.) After the gimmick at Mont Ste. Anne, Quebec, Chretien said, "Looked like a guy in good shape, didn't I." The media agreed and, unlike Day later that year, did not mock him.[179] It is devastating for a politician to be ridiculed. Another media attack on Day that made him look foolish was an on-going segment on the CBC comedy show *This Hour has 22 Minutes*. It was a spoof on the unofficial Alliance policy supporting a referendum on issues when three per cent of the electorate petitioned for one. *This Hour's* website featured a petition calling on Stockwell Day to legally change his name to Doris Day.

Once the vicious invective and mocking dismissal were over and the ballots were counted the Liberals were returned with a larger majority than in '97: Liberals 172, Canadian Alliance 66, Bloc Quebecois 38, NDP 13, PC 12.

The Bloc Quebecois provided a unique option to Quebec voters; during the 2000 election, it became less a nationalist/separatist party than a safe place to "park" a protest vote against the governing Liberals. Jeffrey Simpson says the BQ "represents a handy and cost-free safety valve for francophone Quebecois to express their dissatisfaction with the status quo without having to decide in a federal election their preferred alternative to that status quo."[180]

Because of the way seats in Parliament are distributed, even moderate success by the Bloc Quebecois inside Quebec makes it extremely difficult for any other party to establish itself as a viable national alternative. The Bloc takes nearly half the seats out of play in the province, leaving the other parties, (mainly the Liberals, who have certain established strongholds throughout the province) competing for a limited allotment of seats from Quebec.

The region east of Quebec is the most competitive for the three old-line parties (the Liberals, NDP and PC). The government's payoff to Atlantic Canada with the sweetening of the EI program paid dividends for the Chretien Liberals in 2000. The party nearly doubled its '97 showing, winning 19 of 32 seats compared to just 11 in the previous election.

In the West, the Canadian Alliance solidified its position. The Liberals won 14 seats in the West, with just two each in Alberta and Saskatchewan.

Once again, the Liberals won on the strength of their showing in one province. Ontario delivered 100 of 174 seats the party won. The Chretien Liberals were again the most successful regional party. The lion's share of the Liberal vote came from one region. The "other" 74 seats came from Quebec, in poor and underemployed regions of Atlantic Canada and from some urban seats in the West, notably Winnipeg, Edmonton, and Vancouver. Neither the uninspiring Tories nor the ineffective Alliance seriously challenged the Liberal hegemony. Together, would they have made much of a difference?

Blame for vote splitting in 2000 is attributable to Joe Clark and his Tories, who defiantly opposed any gesture of co-operation[181]. Indeed, Clark openly spurned Preston Manning's invitation to participate in the first United Alternative convention in January 1999. When Reform Party members overwhelmingly approved a proposal to end the party and form the Canadian Alliance, as Peter G. White and Adam Daifallah observed in *Gritlock: Are the Liberals in Forever?*, "only Joe Clark and his band of followers would boycott the move to unite conservatives against the Liberals."[182] Clark would not even give Progressive Conservative party members a chance to voice their opinion on joining the new Alliance through a referendum.

The combined CA-PC vote in 2000 would have produced 36 more seats – 34 from the Liberals and two from the NDP. While the Liberals could have still won, their status in Parliament would have been reduced to a minority government of just 138 seats. The combined CA-PC total would have been 114 seats. While not exactly encouraging for the political opponents of the Liberals, this result would have produced more accountable government for Canadians, and toned down some of the arrogance among the Liberals. White and Daifallah said the divided right, indeed the rivalry between the small-c conservative parties, continued "to yield huge unearned and undeserved benefits to the Liberals" in 2000 as it had in 1997 and 1993.[183] While the thought of uniting the two parties seemed, in practice, little more than an intellectual exercise in the 2000 election, the need for a united opposition is clear when one examines the raw numbers.

While Liberals seemed to have benefited from the division on the right, they were also the beneficiaries of declining voter turnout and nowhere was this as clear as in Ontario. As White and Daifallah note, voter turnout in that province in the federal elections in 1993, 1997 and 2000 dropped precipitously after remaining relatively stable for 50 years. And once the decline had begun in Ontario, the rate of decline was much quicker than that in other provinces. They hypothesize – and with good reason – that a major factor in that decline of voting was a "massive new indifference or even distaste among voters for all the parties and politicians currently on offer."[184] The combined Progressive Conservative/Reform or P.C./Canadian Alliance vote percentages stayed relatively stable from 1988-2000, but the number of Ontarians voting for the conservative side declined in each election. White and Daifallah argue that many Ontario voters became tired of the internecine battle between Tories and Reform/Alliance; that these voters have, in effect, declared a pox on all their houses by simply not voting. (Indeed, some would vote Liberal but considering that the Liberal vote totals – as opposed to their percentage – have also been steadily declining.) It seems voters turned their backs on a political system where they saw on the one hand a tired, possibly corrupt Liberal party devoid of new ideas, and on the other hand two alternative parties which seem more concerned with preserving their own skin and battling each other than with presenting a viable alternative to the Liberals.

Also, just as in 1997, it appears many Canadians stayed home in the 2000 election because they thought their ballot would not make a difference. In the final weeks of the campaign, the polls indicated another Liberal victory. Those polls seemed to show that the Alliance would not be able to break into Ontario in any significant way, which meant that, in practice, the Liberals were guaranteed another win. Because of this perception, many Canadians who were unhappy with the Liberals did not exercise their vote simply because they perceived that doing so would not make any difference to the final outcome. Related to this phenomenon of the inevitability of one party winning the election are people who only want to vote "for a winner" and those who see voting for a losing party as a "wasted vote". Eli Schuster recorded an exchange between nominal supporters of Liberal MP Joe Volpe (Eglinton-Lawrence): "I'm not too happy with Chretien," said one voter. "Who else are you going to vote for?" replied his friend.[185]

Chretien could plausibly claim victory in the 2000 election with gains almost right across the country. The Liberals lost a seat each in BC, Manitoba and Ontario but gained seats in Newfoundland, New Brunswick, Nova Scotia, Quebec, Saskatchewan and the Yukon. Despite fears that they would be wiped out in Alberta, they managed to hang on to both of their Edmonton MPs. Indeed, Chretien increased his majority to 172 seats and the party's popular vote by two per cent. He would read this as a resounding mandate for the status quo.

The election confirmed in the minds of partisan Liberals that they were indeed the Natural Governing Party. There was no credible national alternative with the other five parties entrenched in their particular regions but poised to break free of those regional constraints. Day was demonized, and Chretien assumed the familiar role of the default candidate. Once again, "Canadian values" were safe because of Chretien's leadership.

CHAPTER SIX

LEGACY HUNTING

---

j ean Chretien had achieved political success as no other peace-time federal leader had done in Canada, winning three successive majorities. The Chretien Liberals interpreted this unprecedented triumph not only as an endorsement of the status quo, but also of Chretien's way of doing things. But it is more likely that rather than being a vote of confidence Canadians had chosen the Liberals because they perceived them to be the least objectionable of the available options in the election.

The Chretien Liberals were familiar and predictable, safe and bland. In the big scheme of things, they had done little and the pabulum they offered as vision was easily digestible by a majority of Canadians. Chretien was aware of this. He had won majorities three times without defeat, an impressive political record. Yet there was very little to show for it. After seven years in office, Chretien was finally ready to turn his attention to governing, hoping to enact policies that could serve as his legacy.

After Paul Martin left Cabinet in 2002, Chretien's penultimate throne speech in October of that year was widely expected to be the prime minister's outline for a legacy. Instead, it turned into a rehash of past promises: more money for childcare, healthcare, cities, foreign aid, mass transit, housing, aboriginals and a review of campaign finance and marijuana laws. They were, at heart, the same themes that throne speeches had been earmarking for action in the previous seven years. Political opponents and all but the most Liberal-friendly pundits were exasperated with the last-minute push for a legacy. A legitimate question for Canadians was: what had the Chretien-led Liberals done with their time in government? For fiscal conservatives, if they are honest, the results were not terrible: slightly reduced taxes, balanced budgets, the beginnings of paying down the debt, no grand new multi-billion dollar programs or schemes (except, of course, for the failed gun registry). As David Frum said in 1998, "the dirty secret of contemporary Canadian politics is that from the point of view of right-of-centre Canadians, the Liberals are running really quite a tolerable government."[186]

Modest tax reductions and debt repayment is not the sort of legacy that Chretien, a moderate progressive, wanted for himself. There was no visionary program to satisfy the utopian dreams dancing in Chretien's head. As Michael Bliss observed, "Chretien seemed to have made an unusually small mark on his country."[187] Aside from a few tawdry scandals that the public probably wanted to forget, there was little to remind Canadians of Chretien's time in office.

After nine years as prime minister, Chretien had very little to show for his work and the average person could wonder: why hold power if one is not hoping to do something with it? With the litany of broken promises (scrapping the GST, installing an independent ethics commissioner) and scandals (APEC, HRDC, Shawinigate, Adscam, the gun registry waste, Dupuy), their claim to be competent managers could be reasonably questioned. The answer to the question of what the Liberals had done with their decade in power under Chretien became apparent with the news of the Adscam scandal; they had rewarded friends and tried to influence voters with their own money. Even before the country became aware of Adscam, Canadian Alliance leader Stephen Harper said that, as opposed to the Liberals, the CA had been founded to achieve something: "It was not the lure of power nor the attraction of the spotlight. It was not to pad our resumés, reward our friends or settle the family score. It was to create something that will last, something that will offer tangible benefits to all Canadians." A legacy, Harper continued, "is something that will last. To build one, one must borrow from the experience of the past, deal with the realities and the real problems of today and focus on what we will leave to our children and grandchildren."[188]

Pundits thought that the healthcare report presented by former Saskatchewan premier Roy Romanow in November 2002 would be the basis of a legacy, with some commitment by the Chretien government to secure financing or reform Canada's abominable healthcare system. However, in the 12 months between the release of Romanow's report and Chretien's retirement, there was no new healthcare initiative or funding commitment. Romanow has, in fact, complained about the lack of action by the federal government on his report.

The third mandate provided an inauspicious start for Chretien's quest for a legacy. The first real policy debate of Chretien's third term was a rehash of a policy proposed in 1995, that took effect in 1998 but caused embarrassment to the government: the federal gun registry. It was both a financial sinkhole and an abject failure as a policy.

In fact, the gun registry is the quintessential Chretien boondoggle: after proposing a registry of all rifles and other long-weapons (Canada has had a handgun registry since 1934), the government suspended passing the legislation until it had conducted hearings. Or, more properly, "hearings." Few doubted that the government had made up its mind well before it announced a cross-country hearing tour on the issue. In fact, many observers saw the hearings as a sham; a public relations exercise whose conclusions could have been written before the committee ever hit the road. But the "hearings" found the expected, that Canadians "wanted" a gun registry.

It is dubious that gun registration reduces crime, but the government was adamant that such a program be implemented in Canada. Furthermore, there was no evidence that rifle-murders were a problem; in fact, murders committed by handguns made up an increasing proportion of murders committed by guns.

Such evidence notwithstanding, the government went ahead with its gun registry program, claiming that the system would only cost $2 million after registration fees were factored in; in all, the estimated costs would be $119 million, with fees covering just over 98 per cent of the costs.

By the time the issue made it to Parliament, Justice Minister Allan Rock said the total cost would be $85 million. On February 16, 1995, he told the House of Commons, "We encourage the members opposite to examine our estimates. We are confident we will demonstrate that the figures are realistic and accurate." In 2002, the auditor general found that the Department of Justice had not provided "Parliament with sufficient information to allow it to effectively scrutinize the Canadian Firearms Program and ensure accountability."[189] When Bill C-68 was before the House, the government ignored warnings from more than 20 Reform MPs that the cost estimates for the *Firearms Act* were woefully low and that the eventual cost would be closer to $1 billion.[190]

In her 2002 report, Auditor General Sheila Fraser found that the actual cost was $800 million, criticizing the government's 2002 numbers that the program had cost $688 million; two years earlier, the Justice Department reported the cost to be $327 million but estimated that by the time the program was fully implemented, the cost could reach $1 billion.[vii]

Part of the reason for the upward revisions was, as the Auditor General found, "its original estimates of $5.50 for processing owner licences and $4.60 for processing firearms registrations were too low."[191] By 1998, the actual costs were $23.75 and $16.28 respectively.

The Justice Department was filing so many cost estimates it was becoming almost impossible to keep track of them all, or to believe the department knew what it was doing. In May 1998, it received $544 million from the Treasury Board for the gun registry. By the time it began collecting registration applications in December – just 7 months later – it became clear that the cost assumptions were not valid. It took the bureaucrats in the Justice Department more than a year to inform Treasury Board that they would need more money.

With the numerous revisions, a sign of a total breakdown in accounting procedures at the Department of Justice, Canadian Taxpayers Federation president Walter Robinson had had enough. He called the cost overrun "Enron accounting of gigantic proportions." Later some estimates put the eventual cost at $2 billion. In March 2003, Canadian Alliance MP Garry Breitkreuz said a Library of Parliament research paper indicated the total cost would be a billion dollars more than the billion dollars the Auditor General had determined it to be.[192]

It seemed that the government often low-balled the cost estimate to help sell the gun registry it was intent upon imposing on the nation. For the Chretien Liberals, the program was good for the nation

vii. The Auditor General's report said the Justice Department's estimates did not include the regulatory costs, such as the enforcement costs incurred by the RCMP and the provincial and territorial police (section 10.29).

regardless of the costs. The rationale of the firearms registry is outlined in the Justice Department's 2002-03 *Report on Plans and Priorities*: "to implement a practical approach to gun safety that works to keep firearms from those who should not have them while encouraging safe and responsible gun use by legitimate firearms owners." The problem from a logical point of view was simple, but ignored by the Liberal government: the type of people the gun registry was to prevent from "keep[ing] firearms" would not avail themselves of the gun registry. The criminal class that obtains and uses illegal guns was not going to run to the nearest RCMP station to sign up for the registration program. As Breitkreuz accurately pointed out, the gun registry "concentrates almost exclusively on law-abiding, responsible" gun owners "instead of criminals, gangs, smugglers and terrorists."[193]

It might be argued that a program such as gun registration cannot be judged by its costs. Indeed, in November 2002, Justice Minister Martin Cauchon said in the House of Commons, the registry was "a fantastic value" because it was "protecting our society."

But how well does it protect our society? How do the costs compare to the benefits? Anyone claiming to know how many lives have been saved is making a dubious assertion at best. In 2003, Allan Rock, the former Justice Minister, wondered, "What is the value of 300 saved lives?" But as Peter Stock noted in *The Report*, Rock's calculation was based on a decline from 1,364 firearms deaths in 1989 to 1,006 in 1999. Stock said the "Liberal's licensing program can hardly take credit, since it had not yet been implemented."[194] Furthermore, he reported, the vast majority of gun deaths were suicides. Such a defence of a government program was scandalous, but typical. Having faced a divided and undisciplined opposition for nearly a decade, the Chretien Liberals had lost the ability and the will to debate or defend their policies. There was no need to sink to the level of having to persuade Canadians about the wisdom, necessity, or efficacy of their policies; the

Chretien Liberals knew best and facts and the wishes of the public be damned. The primary reason Canada would have a gun registry was because the Liberal Party was ideologically committed to it.

* * * * * *

Another ideological commitment of many in the party, including the Prime Minister, was the fervent belief that Canada was somehow better or morally superior to the United States. There is nothing inherently wrong with any government promoting a healthy notion of nationalism or national self-esteem, but the ugly anti-Americanism that was used to make the point had serious consequences for US-Canada relations and Canada's role in the post-September 11 world.

After September 11, Jean Chretien was slow to recognize the gravity of the situation and did little to offer the United States any material assistance in the War on Terror. Even the offer of condolences to our neighbour to the south for the losses incurred on that day came too late for many Canadians. Chretien would point to Canadian hospitality in having 224 airplanes en route to the U.S. stay overnight in Canada after the Americans closed their airports and airspace. Canada hosted 33,000 travelers in a time of crisis and confusion. But beyond that and a token military representation in the war on terror in Afghanistan[viii.] it is difficult to see how Canada came to the aid and comfort of our closest ally and biggest trading partner. When 100,000 Canadians assembled on Parliament Hill three days after the terrorist attacks in the United States, the Prime Minister was not among them. The prime minister also took his sweet time to go to Ground Zero, foregoing an opportunity to visit the site of the World Trade Centre terrorist attack

---

viii. Stephen Brown suggested in *Front Page Magazine* that Chretien cynically "decided to send 2,800 troops (almost all Canada has left) to Afghanistan, so that when the bullets start flying in Iraq, he can honestly say he has no soldiers left to send there." ("Canadian Perfidy," FrontPageMagazine.com, March 10, 2003.)

while in the United States to return hurriedly to Canada for a Liberal Party fundraiser.

In a presidential address a few days after September 11, President George W. Bush acknowledged the countries which had risen to stand beside the US in its time of need, but Canada was not included on the list. David Frum, the Canadian-born Bush speechwriter, remembered that his "stomach plunged" as he read a draft of the speech: "All references to Canada had been cut." But as he noted, many other countries were "much quicker than Canada to offer aid and assistance." The "savage and unexpected slap" was meant to signal that the US was displeased that Chretien had not attended the Ottawa vigil, had not joined Australia and the United Kingdom in offering military assistance, and was unconcerned with Canada's lax immigration and refugee laws that practically invited terrorists to enter the US across the two countries' common border. "Canada was omitted [from the speech] because it is easy to forget friends whose governments give you no cause to remember them."[195]

Andrew Cohen says that Chretien did not show the United States that he understood the gravity of September 11: "If he was shaken that day, he was not stirred."[196] More importantly, Cohen ascertains that Chretien's reaction was dictated by his desire not to seem too pro-American.

The issue of Chretien's anti-Americanism came to a head during the lead-up to the war in Iraq. It became obvious well before the US State Department would announce that more than 30 countries were part of the "Coalition of the Willing," that Canada was not to be among them. Chretien noted, rightly, that Canada is allowed to make its own foreign policy. But with the Liberals, this has often manifested itself as taking the road not taken by the Americans.[ix] It is hardly an act of sovereignty when one is forced into a particular policy purely as a display of contrariness. In fact, it could be argued that a nation can lose its sovereignty not only by blindly following the policies of another nation, but that this loss can come equally when there is a blind, stubborn, and ideological determination not to follow that other country's policy purely out of nationalistic spite.

As events unfolded before the war for Iraq, it became painfully clear that the Chretien Liberals were caught in a very tight grip of anti-Americanism.

On November 26, 2002, the *National Post* reported that an unnamed aide to the Prime Minister had called President George W. Bush a "moron." Earlier that year, Oakville, Ontario Liberal MP Bonnie Brown had compared the impending US military action in Iraq to the Japanese attack at Pearl Harbor and Nazi aggression in Europe. This time, however, in the post-September 11 world in which the US tried to ascertain which countries could be counted on as allies in the War on Terror (and which could not), words were watched much more closely, especially when uttered by someone in the PMO. The aide was speaking off-the-record with journalists while on a prime ministerial visit to Prague. Robert Fife, a reporter at the *National Post* had overheard the discussion, and reported it. Although it was almost immediately obvious that Francoise Ducros, Chretien's director of communications, had made the offending remarks, the PMO released this statement: "The Prime Minister's Office never comments on newspaper reports attributed to unnamed sources." Once Ducros was identified as the source, opposition critics called for her resignation and wondered if her comments "reflect the views of the Liberal government."[197] Bush spokesman Ari Fleischer said the comments came from "somebody who obviously doesn't speak for the Canadian government." But as the CBC noted, "The problem is Ducros does speak for the Canadian government, usually on background and off the

---

ix. Lawrence Martin said the Prime Minister also opposed the war because the business community "was avidly pro-war" and Chretien "relished the opportunity to thwart the establishment class."

(Iron Man: The Defiant Reign of Jean Chretien, p. 413)

record."[198] When the pressure became too much, an initially unremorseful Ducros offered her resignation to the Prime Minister on November 26. She did not admit to calling Bush a moron but regretted that a private discussion was now a topic of international conversation. "The comments attributed to me in no way reflect my personal view of the President," she said defiantly as she offered to resign her post in the PMO. At least two reporters, the one Ducros was talking to and Fife, had clearly heard her calling Bush a moron. Chretien initially refused Ducros' resignation saying that he and Bush were friends and that Ducros, if she had used the word "moron", did not do so disparagingly. He said it was a common part of her speech and joked, "She may have used that word against me a few times."

The Canadian Alliance's Jason Kenney called the remark the latest "in a string of anti-Americanism coming from people in senior positions with the Liberal government." As the controversy over the moron remark continued, Ducros again submitted her resignation and finally on November 28, Chretien accepted it. The string of anti-American comments was about to get longer. In the spring of 2003, as the United States started moving into Iraq, Mississauga MP Carolyn Parrish said "Damn Americans, I hate those bastards"[x]. And Natural Resources Minister Herb Dhaliwal called the President a "failed statesman" because he had not found a diplomatic solution through the United Nations. Dhaliwal refused to apologize for the remark and Chretien did not discipline him.

The anti-Americanisms from the Liberal government were starting to be taken seriously south of the border. Paul Celluci, the US ambassador to Canada, responded with a critical speech to a business group in

---

x. Carolyn Parrish also arrogantly threatened reporters demanding that they not to include her anti-American outburst in the stories they filed. Stephen Brown reported in Front Page Magazine that Parrish told a Globe and Mail reporter "that if they reported her comments, not to bother calling her anymore – and that she would work to restrict reporters' access to areas of Parliament." ("Canadian Perfidy," FrontPageMagazine.com, March 10, 2003)

Toronto. Celluci criticized Canada's decision to not participate in the liberation of Iraq, but saved his strongest outrage for the Prime Minister's refusal to discipline members of his caucus for using impolitic and impolite terms for the US leader. Celluci specifically named Dhaliwal.

The MPs and cabinet members took their cue from the top. Chretien's anti-Americanism was well known, even after September 11. Michael Bliss noted, "While Jean Chretien dutifully went through the motions of reaffirming Canadian-American solidarity after 9/11, the extreme woodenness and occasional tardiness of his public gestures suggested they were not issuing straight from his heart."[199]

The White House "reviewed" a May 5 presidential visit to Ottawa that would eventually be cancelled. The anti-Americanism of the Chretien Liberals was beginning to affect the relationship between the two countries that shared the "longest undefended border" in the world and that comprised the globe's largest trading partnership. Noting that more than 85 per cent of our foreign trade is with the US, Canadian Alliance MP James Rajotte asked Chretien: "Why is the Prime Minister putting our jobs and security at risk by tolerating anti-Americanism in his cabinet and in his caucus?" Chretien responded by deflecting the criticism and calling to question the patriotism of his critics by saying that Canada was an independent country that could choose its own course. Noting, "We have the right to disagree with our neighbours," Chretien claimed, "We have done it in good faith." The comments from Brown, Ducros, Parrish, Dhaliwal and Chretien himself indicate that the divergent foreign policy paths were not done in good faith but out of the venal vanities of a second-rate power.

In the aftermath of September 11, cultural critic Robert Fulford called anti-Americanism "one more distortion of the Canadian spirit," adding that after the terrorist attacks in New York and Washington DC, Canada (and others) should realize that on balance, the US influence in the world is more beneficial than harmful and that "accepting this reality means understanding the United States rather than reinforcing prejudices against it."[200] The problem with the comments by senior members of the PMO, the cabinet and the Liberal caucus, was that they reinforced Canada's anti-American prejudices rather than engaging in any serious discussion about the relative benefits or demerits of US influence and policy. Again, smug Liberal attitudes would lead to posturing and flippancy rather than debates about substantive issues.

Chretien's anti-Americanism took an even more self-righteous turn when, at a May 14, 2003 Liberal fundraiser in Quebec, Chretien took a cheap shot against the United States by criticizing Bush's "right wing" administration. Chretien said that Canada's Liberal government was more fiscally disciplined than that of the allegedly conservative Bush administration and noted that if Canada spent money at the rate the US did, it would have a $75 million budget deficit. He then turned his attention to domestic policy differences saying Canada was superior to the US because Canada had gun control, abortion and no capital punishment. "We don't have big debates on the rights of abortion [sic] because we decided a long time ago in Canada it is the choice of women, which is not the case in a lot of US states."[xi.] He added, "That is why we abolished capital punishment, because we believe in a civil society, because we believe capital punishment is not a remedy for social ills."[201] And as Lawrence Martin wrote, Chretien wanted to implement the ultimately flawed gun registry because gun control "was a motherhood issue" for the prime minister. "He had always taken great exception to American gun culture, which he considered the most uncivilized aspect of that great republic."[202]

---

xi. Chretien's comments betray his ignorance of the United States. Abortion is legal in every American state.

It was clear that Chretien wanted, through the promotion of various policies, to turn Canada into the "unAmerica". In some sense it could be argued that he was even entitled to that. However, it was quite another matter to criticize the United States over its domestic policies and arrogantly claim Canadian superiority expressly because of those policy differences. It seemed that the Chretien Liberals were content to govern by clichés.

* * * * * *

Desperate for some legacy as his time in office was quickly running out, Chretien found two issues suddenly available to him: Kyoto and same-sex "marriage." Both would be controversial and, regardless of what one thinks of the policies, poorly handled. The government signed onto the Kyoto Protocol to reduce greenhouse gas emissions (GHGs) to pre-1990 levels in 1997 but never implemented it. On September 2, 2002, Chretien announced during a UN environmental summit in Johannesburg that Canada would pass legislation enacting the Kyoto Protocol by the end of the year. The news caught even members of his own cabinet by surprise. An unnamed aide to one cabinet minister told the *Ottawa Citizen,* "The minister learned about it the same way other Canadians learned about it, and that was by reading the headlines in the newspapers the next day."[203]

Putting aside the issue of whether global warming is actually a problem, whether reducing GHGs would solve that problem, or if Kyoto would be the best way to reduce GHGs – all issues that might have been discussed if the government had permitted a real debate on Kyoto – the government had neither a plan nor a cost analysis for enacting the provisions of the Protocol. Initially, Chretien wanted to ratify Kyoto within a month, but the deadline was pushed back to the end of the year after opposition and backbench MPs said the Protocol deserved at least some Parliamentary debate.

The debate would prove deficient. Liberal backbenchers such as Tony Valeri, Janko Peric and Walt Lastewka urged the Prime Minister to extend his timetable to pass Kyoto. Peric, who supported Kyoto, said industries affected by it were insufficiently consulted. "I would urge the Prime Minister strongly not to rush into" it, Peric said. "We will do it, but, take some time: start involving industry."[204]

Valeri expressed his concern that, as often was the case, MPs were not given the opportunity to have input, to express the concerns of industry and constituents in their ridings. "Parliament should have a role to play," he said, "in what I think is one of the largest undertakings of our government."[205]

Chretien relented, somewhat, and permitted about a dozen hours of debate on Kyoto in a late fall session, but it quickly became clear that the government would not be persuaded to even extend the deadline for ratification. The University of Calgary's David Bercuson and Barry Cooper wrote in a *Calgary Herald* column that, "When measured against other decisions from which the Liberal government has backed away, the Prime Minister's desire to ram through the Kyoto Protocol is a massive anomaly," – that Chretien has almost never acted with "anything like the decisiveness he now is demonstrating on Kyoto."[206] Chretien needed a legacy and he did not want Kyoto to be defeated by Paul Martin's increasingly impatient supporters or delayed by a public debate such as the one that stalled implementation of the gun registry. And what a legacy it would be; Ezra Levant, author of *Fight Kyoto: The Plan to Protect Our Future*, says, "Implementing the Kyoto Protocol is Chretien's plan to elevate himself from a workmanlike politician to a global statesman."[207]

The Chretien push for Kyoto demonstrated all of the ugliest features of the Prime Minister's reign. Kyoto was not about global warming; it was about the political game. As Bercuson and Cooper argued, there were four political elements to passing Kyoto hurriedly: it would cause trouble for Paul Martin whose ambivalence over the issue would lead him to ultimately disappoint supporters; it allowed Canada to be on the opposite side of the US on another policy issue rooted in the "pathological desire to side with the Europeans by disagreeing with the Americans in public"; it reasserted Chretien's and the PMO's commitment to greater centralization at the expense of the provinces by picking "a fight over environmental jurisdiction" and increasing "the scope of their regulatory reach"; and, of course, it would be a central component of Chretien's legacy.[208]

Levant argues Kyoto not only cements Chretien's legacy at home but globally, and at the same time furthers his international ambitions to be a major player on the international stage.[209] It is a sad reflection that Chretien would, in his final days as prime minister, foist a potentially harmful environmental treaty on the country with practically no discussion in Parliament, purely to advance his own standing and legacy.

* * * * * *

Several months before the Kyoto announcement, the Ontario Superior Court had handed Chretien another issue. For several years, the issue of same-sex "marriage" (SSM) had wound its way through the courts. The federal government had defended the traditional definition of marriage as the union of one man and one woman to the exclusion of all others. Homosexual activists and same-sex couples challenged that definition in court. On June 10, 2003, the Ontario Superior Court ruled that the legal definition of marriage was unjustly discriminatory against homosexuals and thus violated their rights under the federal Charter of Rights and Freedoms.

After years of defending the traditional definition of marriage, and despite the fact that his government had supported a 1999 motion expressing opposition to the idea that marriage could be between anyone but a man and a woman, Chretien wrapped himself in the Charter and expressed his desire to see this discrimination end. He prepared legislation that would allow for homosexual couples to marry one another and referred the proposed legislation to the Supreme Court of Canada to see if it satisfied the nine judges' opinion that the new law would be Charter proof.

Opponents castigated the government's acquiescence to a judicially-driven redefinition of marriage. Rory Leishman's description (in another homosexuality-related case) of governments that acquiesce with such court decisions as collaborators[210] is apt in this situation.

Stephen Harper said that the Liberals had expressly permitted the courts to redefine marriage so that they would not get the blame for altering an institution that the majority of Canadians did not want altered. The Liberals and *Toronto Star* scoffed. The *Star* condemned Harper for conspiracy mongering and the Liberals claimed they were only following the orders of the courts. But in June 2003, REAL Women posted on their website photographs of the presiding judges in the marriage case cavorting with top Liberal party strategists and the homosexual activists who had filed the original suit. One of those judges, Justice Heather Smith of the Ontario Superior Court, is married to Senator David Smith who was, until his appointment to the Senate in 2003, a top strategist in the 1993, 1997 and 2000 federal election campaigns and a close ally to Chretien. The Liberals claimed to have no choice but to follow the Ontario court ruling. Of course, that's false. There was clearly an option to appeal the decision to the Supreme

Court, just as the government had done on other lower court decisions that had ruled against the federal definition of marriage. Furthermore, as lawyers for several pro-traditional marriage interveners in the case said, the government did not seem to put its best case forward in defending the law defining marriage as the union of one man and one woman.[xi.] The truth is that they could have mounted a much more vigorous defence of traditional marriage before the courts.

Instead, the Chretien Liberals managed to obstruct a Canadian Alliance motion in Parliament to commit the government to reaffirm the substance of a "defence of marriage" resolution they had overwhelmingly supported just three-and-a-half years earlier. The majority of the Liberal caucus – joined by the NDP, the Bloc and a sizeable portion of the Tory caucus – opposed the motion, which went down to defeat (137-132) in September 2003.

Chretien then proposed redefining marriage to include homosexual couples while promising, "we will protect the right of churches and religious organizations to sanctify marriage as they define it." Calgary bishop Fred Henry warned that Chretien was endangering his own salvation by supporting a policy in direct opposition to the moral teachings of the Catholic Church; Chretien was, in effect, excommunicating himself. Chretien arrogantly dismissed the teachings of the Catholic Church: "[T]he Church does not speak for me." Justice Minister Martin Cauchon drafted three questions for the Supreme Court as part of the government's reference case. The government wanted to know if the way it was attempting to extend marriage rights to homosexual couples – which included exempting churches from the redefinition of marriage – was constitutional. The Official

---

xi. For example, Justice Department lawyers did not even cite Justice Ian Pitfield's 2001 British Columbia decision that found the definition of marriage unalterable because its common law roots precede the Canadian constitution. The failure to note such an important precedent in support of the government's ostensible position seriously calls into question the government's commitment to uphold its own laws.

Opposition, a handful of Tories, many Liberal backbenchers, churches and traditional values organizations criticized the move that took the marriage issue out of the hands of elected legislators and handed it over to the unelected judiciary.

Changes to what many Canadians viewed as the most important and fundamental institution in society would be made, critics noted, without any public input. Indeed, before the Ontario Superior Court had ruled in June, the House of Commons Justice Committee had been holding a series of public hearings across the country to determine how to legally recognize homosexual relationships. When the Court made its decision, committee member Svend Robinson, an openly homosexual NDP MP from British Columbia who had agitated for SSM, filed a motion that the committee accept the Court's decision. The committee voted to accept Robinson's motion. Committee member and Liberal MP Pat O'Brien criticized the committee's action, saying that it was a thumb in the eye of the Canadian public and especially to all those who had participated in the public hearings. The government, in acquiescing in Robinson's motion, shut out public input on this important issue.

The committee's – and the government's – disdain for the views of the majority of Canadians was appalling but typical. Canadians would not be part of the debate on this crucial issue. The move to permit SSM would be a glorious legacy as the Prime Minister left office, even though the Supreme Court ruling would not come until after Chretien had departed the federal scene. But it "fit the leftward lean of his policy-making throughout his last year in office" as it "resurrected the big-L Liberal tradition of Pearson and Trudeau." And unlike most of the other Chretien initiatives – such as distancing Canada from the US or implementing the failed gun registry – moving ahead on SSM would allow Chretien to be "viewed as a prime minister who got things done, as opposed to one who wallowed in political combat and idled on the policy front."[211]

The fact that Chretien needed to be perceived as such a "doer" at this stage of his political career was an unbridled indictment of the past. He'd been involved in federal politics since the mid 1960s, and had been in the PMO for almost a decade. But after all that time, even Chretien himself understood that he was not seen as someone "who got things done." When Stephen Harper asked, "Why does the government not have a legacy after nine years?"[212] the answer was simple: he *had* "wallowed in political combat" for almost a decade to capture and hold onto power for its own sake. Chretien had been so busy destroying enemies and holding off rivals to his power that he had been completely "idle on the policy front."

During Chretien's hunt for a legacy from 2000 to 2003, the only serious distraction was the toughest opponent he would face during his time as prime minister: his own Finance Minister Paul Martin.

With the singular exceptions of the unite-the-right machinations and the Canadian Alliance infighting after the 2000 federal election, the primary political drama of Chretien's ten years in power was the struggle between himself and Paul Martin for control of the party and thus the government. Martin's challenge to Chretien for effective control of the Liberals, and for his hold on the top office in the land, was also the only serious political test Chretien faced. Chretien's hold on the party and the country was dependent upon his ability to keep the private feud from becoming a public one and the personal animosity of that competition from becoming fodder for the stories of political journalists. The heated debate between the two over how the government should handle the broken GST promise – Martin wanted to apologize for an "honest mistake" but Chretien was adamant that they had kept their replacement pledge – would not be fully explored until biographies of the two men were released in late 2003.[213]

The Chretien-Martin rivalry began during the 1990 Liberal leadership race when Chretien, a 27-year veteran of politics who had served in the cabinets of Lester Pearson and Pierre Trudeau, thought that Martin, who had only been elected to Parliament in 1988, should wait his turn; Chretien, his supporters thought, was due. Due is another way of saying entitled. Although Paul Martin finished second and won only about a quarter of the leadership vote, Chretien never forgave the young usurper for opposing him. When the Liberals were elected to government in 1993, Martin did not get the cabinet position for which he had been hoping – a beefed up Industry Ministry where he could have pursued an innovative and activist agenda that would have left its mark on the country. Instead, Chretien wanted to keep his rival close to him (perhaps so he could keep a close eye on him), and appointed him Finance Minister. As Martin's sympathetic biographer Susan Delacourt observed, Chretien thought "ambition was synonymous with disloyalty."[214]

For the first couple of years, the differences between them were hardly noted although generally assumed – Chretien wanted to spend money, Martin wanted to cut spending and create a more friendly business environment in Canada.[xiii.] It was not until the second term that Martin's ambitions became a major headache for Chretien, and the topic of speculation by columnists in the Ottawa press gallery. The caucus was beginning to slowly divide between Chretien loyalists and Martin supporters.

The Prime Minister had too many disappointed supporters – he had a majority of the MPs but only a limited number of cabinet posts to reward them for their loyalty. In his first term, 137 of 172 MPs were not in the cabinet, and the only Martin supporter who did get a post was Saskatchewan's Ralph Goodale.

---

xiii. Numerous off-the-record discussions among journalists and economists with senior bureaucrats and prominent Liberals indicate that Chretien was the one who was adamant about the federal government balancing its budget, not Martin. Although Jeffrey Simpson says in *The Friendly Dictatorship* that one of three modest goals Chretien set for his time in office was to get Canada's fiscal house back in order (p.76), this is not widely reported.

The concentration of MPs from Ontario made the job of handing out political goodies more difficult. This combined with the increased power of the PMO and subsequent unimportance of the backbench, led to a slow but steady rebellion within the Liberal caucus. To a degree, cabinet selection is an exercise in rewarding supporters. But Chretien seems to have taken the loyalty qualification to a new extreme. Lawrence Martin reports a Chretien meeting with numerous Italian-Canadian MPs who were backing Martin. The so-called pasta or spaghetti caucus included Joe Comuzzi, Joe Fontana and Joe Volpe, and they were upset that none of them had been appointed to the cabinet. Chretien, Martin reports, "pointed at each one of them in turn. 'You supported Martin … You supported Martin … You supported Martin'." Chretien noted that two Italian-Canadians, Maria Minna and Alphonso Gagliano, were in the cabinet.[215] Minna and Gagliano were, of course, Chretien supporters. In 2001, an advisor to Chretien suggested the Prime Minister appoint Martin supporter Maurizio Bevilacqua, in Susan Delacourt's words, to "stir up jealousies in the Martin camp, especially among the so-called Italian caucus."[216]

Certainly in the first mandate, Chretien and Martin got along. It could be argued that the government benefited from the Double Vision thesis of two veteran journalists; *Maclean's* Anthony Wilson-Smith and the *Globe and Mail*'s Edward Greenspon argued in their book of the same title, that Canada was guided by the social progressivism of Jean Chretien and Paul Martin's market-friendly balanced budget agenda. Greenspon and Wilson-Smith argue that the two made an extraordinary team in spite of the apparent conflict that existed between them.

No matter how successful it was as policy or politics, the partnership was not to last. Although Martin did not personally go out looking for support among his fellow MPs or at the constituency level, a team of supporters, who had largely stuck with him since the 1990 leadership contest, was organizing on his behalf.[217] Some believed that Chretien would be only a one-term prime minister and then would step aside, leaving Martin as the clear front-runner to replace him. That was not likely to happen but it appears that Chretien did signal to Martin's team that he would step down after being re-elected in 1997.

But three years after that election, when Chretien still did not look like he was headed for retirement, Martin's supporters ratcheted up the pressure for the Prime Minister to step down. The rivalry became a hot topic in political pundit-land and soon, everything that happened in Ottawa was viewed through the lens of the Chretien-Martin rivalry. In an August 3, 1999 cabinet shuffle with a noticeable left-wing tilt, it was noted that the finance minister would not be happy with the government's direction. It was also reported that many MP's who had been skipped over for promotion were Martin supporters.[218] The *Globe and Mail* reported that the shuffle was meant to be a signal to Martin to cool his leadership ambitions because Chretien was probably going to lead the party into a third election.

As the 2000 Liberal biennial convention neared, the Martin team was looking for signals that Chretien would step down. Lawrence Martin reports that there was pressure on Chretien to dump Paul Martin, but that others were afraid this would start a "civil war" within the party.[219] Martin supporters understood that Chretien would step down before the next federal election and that if he would not retire gracefully, they would give him a push out the door. The Prime Minister had turned 65 in January of 1999, an age where many Canadians consider retirement. He had already led the Liberals to two majority governments and he didn't seem to have any ambitious goals left to implement, either personally or policy-wise.

But Chretien had a razor thin, four-seat majority in Parliament, and he had to carefully guard against defections from Martin supporters. For both men, the power struggle for the leadership of the party took precedence over governing as each tried to maneuver for maximum political advantage.

The feud took a new and decidedly unfriendly turn after Martin supporters met at the Regal Constellation in Toronto March 10, 2000 just prior to the biennial party convention. Attending the meeting were numerous Ontario MPs (the so-called "spaghetti caucus" along with Carolyn Bennett, Brenda Chamberlain, Stan Keyes and several others, mostly from southwestern Ontario and Toronto), joined by John Harvard of Winnipeg and Nick Discepola of Montreal. Martin advisors and allies such as aide David Herle, spokesman Scott Reid, and Ontario Liberal strategist Richard Mahoney were also at the meeting, ostensibly called to discuss Paul Martin's "future."[220] Mahoney, the meeting's chairman, presided over a discussion of whether Martin should leave politics. Herle's power point presentation had as its penultimate slide four points including: "We do not believe Chretien has plans to resign," and "We are operating on the assumption that he – like all before him – will hang on to power as long as he can."[221]

The media portrayed – and Chretien believed – the meeting to be preparation for an eventual *coup d'etat*. Lawrence Martin says that Chretien deliberately exaggerated the threat that Martin's supporters posed to party unity to help consolidate his own power.[222] With no real or credible threats from the outside, all the political intrigue was occurring inside the Liberal Party; with no outside enemies, MPs were forced to find them within their own ranks.

Chretien, his biographer claims, had not yet decided to run for a third term. However, it greatly upset him to see Paul Martin's people getting ready for the next election as if their man was already the leader. Jean Pelletier, the Prime Minister's chief of staff, would explain that Chretien had to overcome the perception that he was being pushed out.[223]

Signaling his intention to run again, Chretien hoped to dispel attempts to remove him on anything but his own schedule. And he thought that winning re-election would silence his political opponents within the party. But it was not only Jean Chretien who wanted to run again; his wife Aline was also 100 per cent behind her husband's decision. While watching a CBC report on the Regal Constellation meeting, "Aline clenched her hand into a fist and uttered three simple words: 'Four more years'."[224]

The motivation for the 2000 election call was clear to everyone. During the leaders' debate in November, PC leader Joe Clark looked at Chretien and charged that the only reason he called the early election "was to prevent Paul Martin from getting your job."

The opposition was ill prepared for a November 2000 election, and that certainly played a role in the outcome of the vote. But it appears that Chretien had made up his mind on the idea of an early election primarily as a way to obstruct Paul Martin's prime ministerial ambitions. The opposition's lacklustre election preparedness was just icing on the electoral cake.

In all of this, the business of leading the country took a back seat to the business of desperately holding onto the reins of the Liberal Party. The leadership dispute went beyond the Chretien-Martin feud. Other cabinet ministers were jockeying for a potential leadership run: Sheila Copps, John Manley, Allan Rock and Brian Tobin. With Martin at Finance, he would have the final say (short of Chretien's interference) on what projects would get funding – including those initiated by his potential leadership opponents.

As the Industry Minister, Brian Tobin had developed connections with an array of businesses that could be beneficial during a potential leadership race. He was also considered the most serious challenger to

Martin, and was thought to have Chretien's support once the Prime Minister stepped down. In 2001, Tobin embraced a massive project to make broadband Internet access available across the country. The price tag was a cool billion dollars. The start-up money, he thought, should be announced in the 2002 budget. When the budget was announced, Tobin's internet scheme got just a tenth of the required funding: $105 million, and even that was over several years. Later that year, when both Tobin and Martin were no longer in the cabinet, Finance Minister John Manley and Industry Minister Allan Rock committed themselves to fulfilling Tobin's ambitious Internet agenda.

The conflict between the more activist Tobin and fiscally restrained Martin went back to the Liberal's first mandate, but the budget slight was the last straw.[225] In January 2002, Tobin resigned. This time around, his stay in federal politics had lasted just 16 months. Eventually, the Martin-Chretien rivalry would consume both sides. Tobin's exit necessitated a cabinet shuffle. After January 15 cabinet shuffle, Toronto MP Carolyn Bennett, chair of the Liberal women's caucus, complained that female MPs were not getting the promotions they deserved. Chretien unloaded with a rant against Bennett noting that she was the only MP to dare criticize his cabinet decisions, leading Jeffrey Simpson to joke that the word friendly would be crossed out once the paperback edition of his latest book *The Friendly Dictatorship* was released.[226] An anonymous PMO staffer said to journalists that the only reason Bennett complained was because of her support for Martin. Everything in the PMO was now seen through the lens of the leadership fight. In the spring of 2002, Martin was finally forced out of cabinet, a situation that could have easily become a crisis for the government and the country if Bay and Wall streets had responded negatively. In the end they didn't, but the political maneuvering could have had dire economic and political consequences, with the viability and stability of the Chretien regime called into question.

On May 22, Chretien ordered Martin to end his leadership campaign. Indeed, in an effort not to appear anti-Martin, Chretien tried to put an end to the leadership campaigns of all cabinet ministers, saying they were affecting the governance of the country. For a Prime Minister who was governing based almost exclusively on a cold and calculated analysis of how his actions would help him maintain his own hold on power, it was a little much. Conversations between the PMO and the Finance Minister were becoming heated and there was increased pressure on Martin to either suspend his campaign or leave cabinet. Several Chretien advisors considered it a win-win situation: either Martin would suspend his campaign and thus, (so the thinking went) strengthen Chretien's leadership position. Either that or Martin would be removed from Cabinet, a move that would presumably also get him out of Chretien's hair. As it turned out, both views were shortsighted and wrong.

It later became apparent that after Martin left cabinet, he had considerably more time and freedom to pursue his leadership ambitions. He could (and later evidence bears out that ultimately he did) take control of the Liberal Party on a riding-by-riding, executive member by executive member, MP-by-MP basis. And with Martin's forced departure, the government would lose its most popular minister, the man for whom many Canadians had indirectly voted in 2000.

Negotiations between the PMO and Martin continued but were not going well. Eddie Goldenberg wanted an assurance from Martin that he would remain loyal to the Prime Minister. Returning to Ottawa from his Eastern Townships residence on June 2, 2002, Martin was called by Chretien asking if he had made a decision about his future: was he in cabinet or was he out? Martin hadn't yet decided. Goldenberg then read a letter of resignation from the cabinet, prepared for Martin by the PMO. Martin would not agree to sign it.

Later that day, listening to the car radio en route to Ottawa, Martin learned that John Manley had replaced him as the Finance Minister. Martin hastily called a press conference for the National Press Theatre and, without actually using the word, implied he had been fired. In essence, that's exactly what happened.

It was a calculated risk – if he got the word out immediately, the media would paint Chretien as the villain. The papers and evening news announced that Martin was pushed out of cabinet. Chretien attempted to portray the events differently; the Prime Minister didn't want to be seen pushing the popular Martin out the door against his will. Naming Manley the new finance minister Chretien said, "Mr. Martin and I agreed for the good of the governance of the country that it was better that he was not to be the minister of finance." He went on to claim that he was sad to see Martin leave Cabinet.

Chretien could no longer share the national stage with Martin. The pettiness the Prime Minister displayed in rewarding supporters and punishing the allies of his rivals galled even his fellow Liberals. Lawrence Martin reported that a Liberal Party president, presumably Stephen LeDrew, did not like the Prime Minister's preoccupation in settling factional disputes instead of focusing on the duties of his office.[227] With the Chretien and Martin rivalry, Brian Tobin observed in his autobiography, the Liberal government risked "turning inward to focus on questions of leadership almost exclusively, ignoring the demands and expectations" of governing.[228]

But as Stephen Clarkson noted, for someone who is supposedly so resentful and vindictive, Chretien had co-existed peacefully with his biggest rival since the 1990 Liberal leadership race. This, despite Martin's considerably higher standing among Canadians.[229] Tobin seconds the thought: "In some ways it is remarkable that they made it work so well for so long."[230] This, however, was probably another example of Chretien's realpolitik: keep your friends close and your enemies closer.

Jeffrey Simpson has argued that the rivalry ("sharp policy differences") between the Prime Minister and his finance minister resulted in a "remarkably effective tag-team" with each man's ideas, skills and personalities complementing the other. The effect was that a more socially progressive agenda was implemented under the fiscal restraint of a balanced budget.[231] Delacourt said the policy successes the government had bragged about in its first two terms were the result of "the creative tension between the prime minister and finance minister."[232]

Goldenberg lamented the way Martin left but said it was fortunate it hadn't happened earlier: "The fact that it didn't happen for eight years was pretty good."[233] But Chretien had to remove Martin and prevent a coup if for no other reason than to save himself from being stuck with a lame-duck image. He had things to do.

Because Chretien's ego could not handle the support Martin had received, and because he loathed having his power challenged, the government lost its most competent and most popular cabinet minister. Martin aide David Herle saw his boss' position strengthened after the forced departure from Cabinet. Martin could now openly campaign for the job he had long sought, and Chretien's grasp on power was slipping, according to Herle, for three reasons: "the aimlessness of [the] government, the hardening of Chretien's personality and the inattention paid to all-important political relationships in the past few years."[234] In other words, Chretien's arrogance was finally catching up to him.

CHAPTER SEVEN

THE REAL CHRETIEN LEGACY

---

after a decade in power, Jean Chretien's legacy was, quite literally, scandalous. Cabinet ministers presided over scandals within their departments and were not held accountable for grievously failed policies, misuse of public funds or interference into inquiries and tribunals. The Prime Minister himself was in the centre of numerous questionable government grants and loans to individuals and companies; loans that potentially had a direct bearing on his own financial well-being. And his office had been linked to the obfuscation of numerous inquiries in a desperate attempt to prevent either the Prime Minister or the Liberal Party from having their images sullied. Power was further centralized in the Prime Minister's Office, not to coordinate the implementation of an agenda but to consolidate Chretien's power.

While the Prime Minister frantically sought a legacy – some kind of federal program or accomplishment that would cement his place in Canadian history – there were several less flattering historical footnotes and political trends for which he would long be remembered: the litany of scandals, ever-decreasing voter turnout, a stifling of political debate, the centralization of power and the trivialization of the office of the prime minister by reducing it to being the highlight of a long *curriculum vitae*.

It is surprising the Chretien Liberals got away with it. They came to power promising a much more ethical government than the one they had replaced and the tools (an independent ethics commissioner) to deliver on that promise. On the day that the Chretien cabinet was sworn in, Mitchell Sharp lectured the new government on ethics. To Brian Tobin, the former cabinet minister, this was proof of how seriously Chretien took ethics.[235] It appeared to be little more than window dressing for the MPs and the public; or perhaps, the lessons didn't stick.

In hindsight, Chretien's strategy of denying any wrongdoing, excusing the misconduct, complicating the issue and then finally moving on – denial, deflection and defiance – worked. He would deny the wrong-doing was a breach of ethics, then he would try to deflect criticism by saying the breach was excusable because there were larger issues at stake, then he would ensure that no one understood the issue either by blocking honest inquiries or failing to answer questions and then he would move on (often to the next scandal).

Chretien's strategy in dealing with any scandal was to set the ethics bar so low that virtually anyone in government could step right over it and then proceed to stroll along as though nothing had happened.

While not very controversial at the time, the government's approach to policy-making and its utter contempt for democracy – either for MPs, Parliament, or Canadians – would turn out to be a legacy for Chretien as scandalous as the Airbus and APEC affairs, Shawinigate, and the closing down of the Somalia inquiry. Power was concentrated in the centre, the Prime Minister's Office, to the detriment of not just MPs but also to the detriment of the Cabinet system. All significant policy initiatives either originated in or were ushered through Parliament by the PMO.

Parliamentary democracy does permit a government to enact legislation without much debate, but in practice it is considered undemocratic. The successive governments led by Jean Chretien were not interested in proposing ideas and having MPs discuss them. The PMO heavy-handedly ushered legislation through the process, pressuring, if not outright ordering, Liberal MPs to vote as the Prime Minister wanted. The only serious defeat Chretien suffered in 10 years in office was a vote in 2003 when Paul Martin's supporters backed the efforts of the opposition to have committee chairs chosen by secret ballot, thus reducing the power of the PMO to influence or even bully MPs to support the prime minister's chosen candidates. The opposition and Martin's supporters saw no need for the prime minister to appoint Parliamentary committee chairs considering the extensive appointment power he already enjoyed in other areas.[xiv.]

* * * * * *

With little to show for a decade in power, evidenced by the last minute rush for legacy legislation, it was obvious that Chretien's primary motivation for wanting to be prime minister was power; power for its

---

xiv. Jeffrey Simpson lists the prime minister's appointments: the cabinet, deputy ministers, parliamentary secretaries, the Governor General, the justices of the Supreme Court of Canada, the clerk of the Privy Council, the auditor general, the information commissioner, the ethics counsellor, the heads of Crown corporations and government agencies, ambassadors, senators, and until 2003, the chairman of all Parliamentary committees. Simpson says the Speaker of the House of Commons "aside, everyone of importance in the Government of Canada directly or indirectly owes his or her post to the prime minister." (The Friendly Dictatorship, p. 15.)

own sake. He did not necessarily want to do anything with the power than *to be able* to wield it. Journalist John Gray observed that, "with the exception of … his commitment to keep Quebec within Canada, he has no apparent political vision." Gray continued: "For Chretien politics is about winning, and beyond that there seems scant purpose."[236] So it was not surprising that Chretien accelerated the trend that Donald J. Savoie identified in his seminal book, *Governing from the Centre: The Concentration of Power in Canadian Politics;* the trend of centralizing all federal power directly in the Prime Minister's Office. Those who have power seldom want to share it.

Pierre Trudeau famously said MPs were nobodies 100 feet outside Parliament and he treated them as such. It was Trudeau who had begun the process of consolidating power in the PMO, and Brian Mulroney accelerated the trend,[xv.] but the influence and power of the office reached its apex under Chretien. Whereas in 1928, the Prime Minister's Office had 12 staff members, under Chretien, the communications department alone had 14 and it took 84 people to staff the entire PMO.[237] One staffer defended the size of the office, pointing out that it was smaller than under Mulroney. However, it was not merely the size, but more specifically the influence of the PMO that became a concern. As former Progressive Conservative MP Patrick Boyer said, for the government, "MPs have basically fulfilled their purpose on election night."[238] He meant that aside from giving the government (the executive, or the cabinet) a mandate and the votes to implement a legislative agenda, MPs are not needed except to let their constituents know what the government is doing.

Under Chretien, MPs were rarely engaged in the policy-making process. In fact, in some instances they heard about new government

---

xv. The Chretien Liberals identified Mulroney's use of the PMO as so problematic that the 1993 Red Book promised to reverse this trend, condemning the former prime minister's "arrogant style of leadership" and noting "people are irritated with governments that do not consult them."

initiatives at the same time as the rest of the country. In January 2000, Industry Minister John Manley announced that the government would assist Canada's financially ailing National Hockey League teams. The policy, a relatively insignificant $3 million program, was crafted by the PMO and Industry Canada without Manley's knowledge or approval. But the PMO had Manley trying to sell the ultimately disastrous policy to the public. The plan was quickly rescinded after a huge public outcry about funding "millionaire players and multimillionaire owners" as the critics put it. Susan Delacourt reported that the miscue and particularly the failure to communicate with MPs "seemed yet another example of the PMO cutting itself off from the caucus."[239] If the PMO had communicated its intentions to MPs, it might have avoided the public relations disaster of proposing a policy and then being forced to back down. Simple consultation with MPs would have let the government know in advance that there was little appetite among voters for the notion of having government directly subsidize professional sports of any kind.

Not only did Chretien not engage in policy discussion in Parliament or in public, he ran his caucus and cabinet meetings with little debate about ideas or policy. That is, under Chretien, it was not just MPs who saw their role diminished, but cabinet ministers as well. Savoie called the PMO a "mini cabinet" although Trudeau said in the late 1960s when he enlarged the PMO that it would remain an entity that served, not advised the prime minister. For Chretien, it would neither serve nor advise; Michael Bliss said Chretien treated his cabinet like a focus group.[240]

Oddly enough, Paul Martin was the only one of Chretien's cabinet ministers who had free reign to do what he wanted. Of the two most important policy files under Chretien, Martin handled the budget and the PMO handled national unity.[241]

An aide to one cabinet minister told the *Ottawa Citizen* that when Chretien announced in South Africa in September 2002 that the government would enact Kyoto by year's end, "There was no previous discussion, indication, suggestion, heads-up in any way that the announcement was going to be made, or that it was going to be made in Johannesburg."[242]

Not only were cabinet ministers next to irrelevant in the Chretien regime, having little influence in the government's policy-making, they appeared to have little control over their own departments. Under Chretien, the PMO had vetted senior staff for cabinet ministers and appointed the deputy ministers. An unnamed member of the PMO staff assured the cabinet that, "We will not impose anybody on a minister, but we can veto."[243] Gordon Robertson, a former clerk of the Privy Council, expressed serious concern about the influence of the PMO and the state of Canadian democracy. In 2002, he said the PMO's influence over cabinet might actually be unconstitutional because the Constitution invests executive power in the Governor General with the advice and consent of the cabinet. "I don't think now we really genuinely have an effective cabinet system."[244] Just as it is said that the government viewed MPs as little more than information agents to get the government's message out to Canadians, Chretien saw his cabinet serving him personally as well. In his first cabinet meeting, Chretien is reported to have said that for the "good of the government," cabinet ministers would have to do all they could to protect themselves from "screw-ups" but more importantly, in the words of Savoie, "they should always strive to protect the prime minister."[245]

In *The Friendly Dictatorship*, Jeffrey Simpson noted that senior prime ministerial aides did not consult with ministers about portfolio assignments and that ministers had little influence over policy once they were given their assignments. "Since only the prime minister can play on any file, his advisors [the PMO] can range over the entire ambit of government, ensuring that his bidding is done and his interests are protected."[246] This inevitably leads to what Simpson describes as the "imperial prime ministership."[247]

Besides the PMO, there were two other groups that had a disproportionate share of influence and power at the expense of MPs and cabinet ministers. The Privy Council Office and the Coordinating Group of Ministers (CGM). The latter was a small committee comprised of prominent cabinet members that advised Chretien and Paul Martin. Interestingly, it was Chretien who decided who would be on that committee. Equally telling is the fact that the proceedings of the CGM were vetted by the PMO.[248] Several cabinet ministers resented the power of the CGM. When the Group was advising Martin in 1994 on spending cuts for the 1995 budget and setting spending reduction targets for each department, Agriculture Minister Ralph Goodale said of the CGM: "What gives you the right to act as judges on what generations of other people have created? From what divine right do you derive the power to decide that fifty of my scientists will be without work tomorrow?"[249] The answer to the question 'by what right' was none other than Jean Chretien, and the fact that he had appointed the committee, and that it was doing his bidding.

In an *Ottawa Citizen* series on the state of democracy in Canada, Donald Savoie said the centralization of power is good if the goals are efficiency, decisiveness and bold leadership, but dangerous if the goals preclude regional and public input.[250]

The role of MPs had certainly changed in recent years. Instead of representing their riding in Ottawa, many members of parliament now see their jobs as representing the government in their riding. Given that trend, it is not surprising that many voters have turned away from the electoral process. And this leads to another reason the Liberals were able to realize their base ambition of just holding onto power:

low voter turnout. Many Canadians who were fed up with the Liberals became disengaged politically, registering their disgust with politics by not voting.

During Chretien's reign, voter turnout declined precipitously.[xvi] Just a little more than six in 10 registered voters cast ballots in the 2000 federal election – the lowest percentage in Canadian history. And that number was a full ten percentage points lower than it had been when the Liberals were first elected in 1993.

From 1953 to 1993, only twice did voter turnout fall under 70 per cent: in 1953 the turnout was 68 per cent, and 1980 it was 69 per cent. In both of the elections called by Chretien, voter turnout fell: to 67 per cent in 1997 and 61 per cent in the year 2000.[xvii]

Voter turnout is likely to be lower when the result is a foregone conclusion, as it was in 1997 and 2000. Peter G. White and Adam Daifallah wrote, "In an electoral system that offers no real hope of a change in government, many Canadians see no point in voting at all."[251] Or as the authors of *Unsteady State* found, voter turnout is generally low when there is "no real race for who would form the government."[252]

This was confirmed in Ontario where the Liberal grasp is strongest and where turnout is falling faster than in any other province. White and Daifallah point out that between 1935 and 1988, voter turnout in the

---

xvi. For the record, I do not think that low voter turnout is necessarily a negative phenomenon. However, low voter turnout can be a symptom of a real problem if voters are dropping out of the electoral process because they've given up or they see virtually no chance of replacing a sitting government.

xvii. With turnout declining, many Canadians smugly point to better rates of voter turnout in Canada compared to south of the border where just 50 per cent of eligible voters cast ballots in presidential elections. However, as Jeffrey Simpson notes, our 61 per cent is much closer to their 50 per cent and the sense of "moral superiority," is, "as usual ... misplaced," because the two countries count turnout differently: Canada tallies its totals based on voters compared to the number of people registered on registration lists whereas the United States compares voters to number of eligible voters. Simpson says, if Canada used the same criteria as the United States, "the 2000 election turnout would have been only 51 per cent, or about the same as for the 2000 U.S. presidential election." (Simpson, *The Friendly Dictatorship*, p. 139-140.)

province averaged 75.5 per cent, the fifth highest in the country; indeed, it was still hovering around the three-quarters mark in 1988 (74.6 per cent). "But starting in 1993, Ontario voters have increasingly stayed home in droves."[253] From 1988 to 1993 voter turnout fell 6.9 points to 67.7 per cent, below the national rate of 71 per cent. In 1997, it fell again, to 65.6 per cent, compared to a national rate of 67 per cent. By 2000, it was a mere 58 per cent in Ontario.[xviii] White and Daifallah observe that after remaining stable for 50 years, turnout in Ontario declined 16.6 per cent over the course of three elections.[254]

While the percentages are close – 58 per cent in Ontario compared to a national rate of 61 per cent – Ontario's disproportionately large population had an undue statistical influence in driving down the national rate.

Contrarily, in 1997, voter turnout was highest in New Brunswick and Nova Scotia where there were generally three-way races among the Liberals, NDP and Progressive Conservatives.

All the parties lost support as vote totals declined (generally) across the board.[xix]

White and Daifallah say that "[i]t is misleading to claim … that Ontario is having a mad love affair with the Liberal Party while rejecting all other suitors."[255] They note that the *number* of Ontarians voting Liberal has declined steadily since 1993, from 2,383,065 in '93 to 2,294,593 in '97 and 2,292,075 in 2000.[256] One reason for this is the widely held view, in Ontario at least, that the Liberals will ultimately win both the national election and the local seat. Another reason for the decline in Liberal votes is a backlash against the types of campaigns

xv. Only Newfoundland had consistently lower voter turnouts than Ontario in the 1990s.
xvi. The exception was the re-made Canadian Alliance which saw a numerically significant but ultimately meaningless increase in 2000 from the Reform vote in 1997

the Liberals engaged in: nasty, personalized attack campaigns at the expense of serious, substantive debate on the issues.

Furthermore, as the authors of *Unsteady State* observe, voter turnout is lower when there is no compelling issue.[257] It is partly the fault of the Liberals that no such over-riding issue animated either the 1997 or 2000 election campaigns. Both times, the governing Liberals went to the polls not so much to get a mandate to accomplish anything new (campaign statements notwithstanding) but merely to extend their reign. Secondly, the Liberals focused the campaigns on the question of leadership. And they did so unfairly by trying to present Jean Chretien as a battle-tested Prime Minister and a man with a moderate image, compared to untried and politically extreme, even potentially "dangerous" opponents. The Liberals ran perfectly executed negative campaigns devoid of serious policy discussion. Thus, on election day, there was no issue, such as free trade in 1988, that would have animated people to go to the polls.

A variation of this theory is that voter turnout is lower when the public does not perceive there to be any "meaningful choices."[258] If voters don't see stark differences among the parties, or if the parties fail to sell what distinguishes them from the others, many voters will decide it makes little difference who wins, and they'll ultimately stay home. Despite the heated rhetoric attacking Day as an extremist, the Alliance, Liberal, and PC parties all hugged the centre, offering fiscal restraint, moderate tax cuts and a commitment to pay off the debt. What little policy debate there was did not offer sufficient reason to replace the Liberals.

The Chretien Liberals engaged in relentless character assassination but offered voters nothing themselves; in essence, the Liberals were willing to be the default choice, fashioning themselves as the "devil you know" or the "lesser of two evils." They sought not so much to attract voters to themselves as much as to drive people away from their opponents.

The combination of turning the public off their opponents and running a campaign devoid of any concrete policy ideas gave voters very little reason to go to polls. Declining voter turnout, though, is hardly a problem for governing parties if the numbers work in their favour. "The decline scarcely ripples the conscience of the governing party," Jeffrey Simpson observed. "They won, and that is all they need to know."[259] In fact, if voter turn-offs – negative campaigning, the lack of any serious policy debate – actually depress voter turnout while continuing to deliver Liberal MPs, so much the better. The "problem" of low voter turnout, or of disengagement with politics in general, is not a problem at all for the Liberals; indeed, it has helped them. If the decline in voter turnout was a deliberate result of specific Liberal strategy, this can clearly be seen as yet another example of the Liberal Party cynically putting its political self-interest ahead of what is best for the country.

The Chretien legacy is the scandal of substituting pure and calculated political opportunism in the place of the principle of governing for the good of an entire nation. More than any Canadian administration in modern history, the successive Chretien governments put pettiness and personal politics above the responsibilities of governing. The Liberals under Chretien had truly begun to view themselves as the Natural Governing Party, and their behaviour often betrayed this attitude. And part of the problem was that they considered their "right to govern" to be rooted in their own goodness as contrasted to the evil of their political opponents. They also convinced Canadians of this notion. Stockwell Day was not to be merely defeated in an election through an honest exchange and debate about ideas or political philosophies. Because Liberals considered his views "evil", "dangerous", or even "unCanadian", he had to be utterly destroyed – both politically *and* personally. And this pit-bull style of attack politics wasn't just confined to election campaigns. Anyone who dared oppose or speak out against the Chretien agenda – be it Stockwell Day, members of the APEC complaints review board, or commissioners on the Somalia inquiry – was fair game for personal attack in the relentless, brazen pursuit of power.

It is understandable that Chretien would not want the long list of scandals to be his legacy, but it is these for which he will be most remembered. Pierre Trudeau envisioned a "Just Society". Whether he delivered is still open to dispute. But he will be remembered for trying. Jean Chretien delivered not a "Just Society", but instead a "Corrupt and Ugly Political Culture." This culture included political bullying, personal attacks, nonchalance in the face of adversity, and most of all his smug belief that he embodied all that was good in Canada simply because he survived the endless questions about his ethics. The extent to which these traits were displayed by successive governments under Chretien was unprecedented in modern Canadian history. Only time will tell whether the Liberal Party continues to operate under this kind of hubris.

When Canadians voted in 1997 and 2000, they did not seem to consider that the Chretien Liberals appeared to stand for nothing more firmly than the arrogant belief that only they could (or should) be entitled to govern. And this belief was not rooted in any grand vision for the future, but rather in the nebulous notion that somehow their party embodied "Canadian values".

Indeed, the Liberals sold as "Canadian values" some of the very things that opponents criticized as unprincipled. The fact that the Liberals didn't seem to stand for anything was sold as a virtue. They were "willing to listen" and be "open-minded" and "tolerant". Anyone who *did* hold to any firm beliefs on policy was criticized as being "doctrinaire" and, by implication, "unCanadian." Many Canadians who expected major changes after the Mulroney years were sorely disappointed with the Chretien Liberals and their about-face on Mulroney policies such as free trade, and the adoption of Reform Party principles of spending cuts to balance the budget.[260] It was especially upsetting to small-l liberals that social programs were among the first to go under the spending guillotine in the drive to reduce the deficit. Chretien and his party had explicitly promised to protect those social programs from the threat of the fiscal conservatives in the PC Party. But while their critics said they were duplicitous and hypocritical, the Liberals claimed to be flexible and adaptable to the circumstances, practicing "Canadian values" such as moderation and open-mindedness. The Liberals quite openly acknowledged they had changed course on some of those issues. But they dressed it up as consultative politics, claiming they were willing to adopt the best ideas of their opponents. Those opponents knew, however, that all of this was done with the calculated idea of undermining them in the next election.

Chretien's government proved what many Canadians have long believed – an unpleasant truth best summed up by Will Ferguson: "The Liberal Party is in the business of staying in power."[261] But overly forgiving and willingly blind Canadians were persuaded to see all of those moves as non-ideological, moderate politics.

Indeed, all the scandals, the lack of true policy debate, and the diminution of democracy were all aspects of the single greatest scandal: the obsession with keeping Chretien in power at all costs.

So, the question is, why did Canadians let the Liberals get away with it?

There is no single overriding reason why voters ignored the scandals, patronage and lacklustre leadership to reward Chretien and his party's raw ambition. But Canadians do have to take some responsibility for keeping the corrupt Chretien Liberals in power for a full decade. It was one thing for Canada to ignore the broken promises and ethical indiscretions in Chretien's first term, but the government was re-elected to a third term in 2000 even *after* the Auditor General had released a scathing report on the lack of accountability at the HRDC, and *after* Shawinigate had become a matter of the public record. By this time, Chretien had demonstrated repeatedly his inability or utter lack of interest in holding his government accountable for its mistakes. In that sense, by the 2000 election, Canadians were complicit in the corruption and in aiding and abetting Chretien's personal pursuit of power. Fool Canadians once, shame on the Chretien Liberals; fool Canadians twice, shame on them.

Put another way, as Andrew Coyne wrote in the *National Post* after the Shawinigate affair: Canadians decided that the corruption, the lack of accountability and real conflict of interest guidelines, and the "neutering" of Parliament just didn't matter. But, warned Coyne, if the public says those things don't matter, "we should know we are also saying that democracy doesn't matter; that we are content to be ruled, rather than governed." If that is the case, Coyne said, "we deserve everything we get."[262]

It seems that Canadians were content with the pabulum fed to them by the Chretien Liberals. Denyse O'Leary, a Toronto journalist, once explained that Canadians don't like confrontation because they are so darned polite. Elections are about choices and, unfortunately, choices mean confronting the ramifications and consequences of several alternatives. O'Leary posits the notion that in the 1990's, Canadians collectively settled on the Liberals to avoid confrontation.[263] They did so not only during election campaigns, but also between elections. The attitude seems to be: "steady as she goes, make the decisions, involve patronage if you must but don't interrupt the lives of ordinary Canadians who want to go on with their everyday existence". Jeffrey Simpson said Chretien's "leitmotif" was "the avoidance of trouble … never engaging Canadians in serious debates."[264] Canadians apparently liked it that way.

The historians J.L. Granatstein and Norman Hiller in their brief book examining the legacies of all the prime ministers beginning with Sir John A. McDonald found that Chretien did little to excite the public imagination and that such a minimalist approach to government both limited what he did in office and paradoxically also explained his success. They say that Chretien "apparently had no great abiding vision for the country apart from his passion for it."[265] As a result he took no risks but governed competently, they found, much as Mackenzie King had.[266]

Chretien offered a non-ideological approach to governing. He was not seen establishing a Just Society (Trudeau) nor as dismantling the state (Mulroney), although he sought to do the former as he was doing the latter. He was viewed as centrist.[267] But his was not a philosophical centre as much as it was a stylistic centre. As Peter C. Newman described it: "He seems to define the political centre not so much as a firm philosophical position as that welcome point in the ideological spectrum where he is being attacked from both the left and the right."[268]

He has always lacked vision. He has never really challenged established convention. Newman said that reviewing Chretien's performance since he was first elected (when John F. Kennedy was still president) through nine different cabinet posts, as Leader of the Official Opposition and finally as prime minister, "it quickly becomes clear that most of his policy initiatives have consisted of mildly groping towards orthodox solutions."[269] In other words, he has made "don't rock the boat" his predominant philosophy.

Lawrence Martin said it was commonly understood that, "power always interested him more than the uses to which it could be put." Policy, Martin said, was "a sideshow to the main action, which was political warring."[270] It didn't matter much if the political drama was a battle with Brian Mulroney, Stockwell Day or Paul Martin.

There are numerous other reasons Canadians returned the Chretien Liberals to office. It must be noted, however, that with voter turnout at just 61 per cent in the 2000 election and the Liberals garnering only about 40 per cent of that vote, their mandate was based on the approval of just one in four Canadians who were registered to vote. So perhaps the better question is: why did the one-quarter of Canadians who voted for the Chretien Liberals in 2000 not have any problem returning a corrupt and arrogant government to office? There are at least nine reasons Canadians forgave the prime minister and his government.

1. The Chretien Liberals were perceived to be better than the alternatives. Whether or not the vote was an affirmation of the government's performance, or voters thought "better the Liberal devils we know than the other devils we don't" is impossible to know. Columnist Ted Byfield was persuasive when he argued that given the choice in the 2000 election between two "scary options", the overt Christianity of Stockwell Day or the equally overt sleaze of Jean Chretien, voters chose the second because "they were more comfortable with sleaze, not because they necessarily favoured it, but because it seemed familiar and predictable." No one, it seemed, was quite sure where Day's "Christianity" might lead the nation.[271]

2. Chretien benefited from low expectations. Possibly due to a combination of his facial disfigurement, his speech problems, his mangled syntax and the idea that it had been Paul Martin and not he (Chretien) who was responsible for the upturn in the country's economic fortunes, the public did not expect much from Chretien himself.

3. After a quarter century of Trudeau and Mulroney, Chretien's non-confrontational, non-flamboyant style worked. And because they did not consider the scandals as directly affecting their lives, Canadians didn't worry about them. Compared to his reviled predecessor Brian Mulroney, Canadians did not (and indeed still *do* not) consider Chretien particularly corrupt or arrogant.

4. No more constitutional wrangling. Under Chretien's watch, Canada seemed to finally achieve peace on the national unity issue.
5. Finance Minister Paul Martin got the country's financial house in order and voters did not want to lose their popular and successful finance minister. They somehow separated the finance minister from the rest of the Chretien government.
6. Chretien went into office as someone Canadians liked; they were predisposed to forgive him. Voters connected with Chretien because of the carefully cultivated image of "the little guy from Shawinigan"; unlike the slick and successful businessman, Brian Mulroney, who stepped into the prime minister's office, Chretien "fought" to get where he was. Whatever faults the government had simply reinforced the notion of Chretien's "regular guy" image; we all make mistakes.
7. Voters, especially those in Ontario, want "Trudeau-style centralism" as Link Byfield once noted.[272]
8. As Clark-era cabinet minister and failed 2003 Tory leadership candidate William Heward Grafftey has noted, Shawinigate and APEC did "not constitute the stuff that overthrows governments."[273] While it was clear to all that at the very least Chretien committed "some indiscretion," Grafftey correctly observed that Canadians still felt that their prime minister was "a fundamentally honest man." Or perhaps, more accurately, voters did not consider misappropriation of money and power legitimate issues on which to be making their voting decisions.
9. Voters put aside concerns they had with the Prime Minister and/or his government and cast a ballot for the local MP.

It's unclear whether these are "explanations" or "excuses", but they certainly seem to sum up why it is that voters who knew how corrupt the government was, repeatedly demonstrated at the ballot box that they really did not care about that corruption. It is apparent that, fundamentally, Chretien's strategy for dealing with the repeated scandals worked. People were somehow convinced by the repeated cycles of denial, excuse, deflection, obstruction and confusion. They kept voting Liberal.

This continued support provided the stamp of approval to Chretien's corruption, arrogance, and poor government. The 2000 election majority win for Chretien came one month after the irregularities at the HRDC became public, and in the middle of the Shawinigate controversy. In a democracy, the ultimate accountability comes in the form of a potential electoral defeat. That restraint was always the best cure for corruption. Politicians, worried about not being re-elected, would police themselves and avoid the scent of scandal so they could get re-elected. But as Ted Byfield noted after the 2000 election, "every restraint on outright corruption has now been removed."[274]

While no one can deny that Chretien had electoral success, the toll that success had on the Liberal Party is a concern not only for the party's political opponents but also for many Liberals themselves. Long-time Liberals also worry (quietly) about the effects of Chretien's cavalier governing style, not just on the Liberal Party but also on the country as a whole. Brian Tobin has said he is "uncomfortable about the extended dominance of our party on a national basis, and the inability of any single party to appeal to multiple regions of the country." He said that Canada needs a rejuvenated Conservative Party and NDP. He said that Liberal hegemony is good for the party only in the short-term because, as with a free enterprise business model, strong competition would make the Liberal Party stronger. "Nothing strengthens a party's effectiveness more than facing a well-prepared Opposition."[275] When he was still the party president, Stephen LeDrew fretted that a party that dominated politics as the Liberals had in the 1990s and early 2000s, where "there was no effective parliamentary opposition" would, "like a bunch of soldiers … [with] no enemy to shoot," begin "taking target practice" on themselves. He characterized the Chretien-Martin feud during the Prime Minister's long run-up to retirement as precisely such a shoot-out.[276]

The conflict with Paul Martin, and especially Chretien's almost pathological need to hold on to his office at all costs, besmirched the office of the Prime Minister. By putting his own selfish desires ahead of the needs of the country and using his office to settle petty, vindictive and personal grievances, Chretien trivialized and denigrated the most important political position in Canada. The power the prime minister has – the thousands of appointments, directing the national agenda, representing the country abroad – all these things were subsumed to the need to satisfy one man's ego.

The scandalous history of the Chretien Liberals is only touched upon in this volume. There are many more examples that demonstrate how Liberal governments from 1993-2003 served their own interests rather than those of Canadians. At the risk of writing the longest run-on sentence in the history of the English language, here's a partial list of the most obvious ethical lapses to occur on Chretien's watch: the cancellation of the Pearson Airport deal, which cost taxpayers hundreds of millions of dollars purely to satisfy Chretien's vanity; the George Radwanski affair, in which the Privacy Commissioner used his office budget to live luxuriously; cabinet ministers being less than truthful about their fully funded stays at the Irving fishing lodge in the Maritimes; Marcel Masse's role in having Liberal fundraiser Pierre Corbeil approach companies seeking federal grants to donate to the Liberal Party in Quebec; Alphonso Gagliano's department granting contracts to Gagliano's son; the purchase of new Challenger jets for Jean Chretien while the Canadian military continued to go begging for replacements for its outdated and dangerous Sea King helicopters; Defence Minister Art Eggleton awarding a $36,500 untendered contract to an ex-girlfriend; HRDC minister Gagliano instructing a crown corporation to put his speechwriter Michelle Tremblay on retainer; the spending habits of Sheila Copps' aide Charles Boyer; Finance Minister John Manley lobbying the CIBC on behalf of then Ottawa Senators owner Rod Bryden at a time when the CIBC was hoping the finance ministry would permit bank mergers; MP Gerry Byrne pouring Atlantic Canada Opportunities Agency money into his own riding while he was the minister responsible for the regional development program; the granting of OCOA contracts to a brother of another minister with responsibility for the program, Robert Thibault; the untruthful claim that Paul Martin's company, Canadian Steamship Lines, had won government contracts worth just a few million dollars when the real number was $161 million; the patronage appointment of convicted tax evader and former Trudeau-era cabinet minister Roger Simmons to the post of Consul-General in Seattle; the awarding of contracts to a public relations firm to promote an event *after the event had already taken place*, (the firm was run by an associate of MP Maria Minna and two days after the contract expired, that associate became her campaign manager); Transport Minister Herb Dhaliwal overseeing the potential funding of new transit lines in and out of the Vancouver airport, on a route that would be in direct competition with his own limousine company; the doubling of the Governor General's budget in five years, mostly for travel and the maintenance of other lavish lifestyle perks. The list could go on, but the point has been made.

Considering all this, how did a seemingly inept and perhaps corrupt prime minister hold the confidence of the Canadian public? Chretien governments experienced at least as many scandals as those of Brian Mulroney. The former Tory prime minister is still reviled by many Canadians, while Chretien is simply considered a rather likeable but bumbling leader.

There is no doubt that Chretien was a Teflon prime minister. Nothing stuck to him. Discussing Chretien's popularity following his re-election in 1997, Peter Newman described the prime minister's seeming endless popularity:"Ordinary Canadians believe he is one of their own, instead of one of those blow-dried elitists who run the country according to their own smug, self-serving agendas."[277] Chretien biographer Lawrence Martin returns to this theme of Chretien being "the little guy from Shawinigan" to explain the man's longevity in the corridors of power. But the "little guy" thing was clearly just an image; after almost four decades in elected office, most of them in cabinet or other senior positions of government or opposition, Chretien could not credibly claim to be a regular guy fighting to stay at the top. He had been at the top for too long and that made him arrogant. He was beyond reproach, and shameless in his quest to stay in power; the little guy became a little tyrant obsessed with power.

By the end of his decade-long tenure as Prime Minister it was clear that he was where he was to serve himself and his party rather than the country. Chretien, as demonstrated by the events following his departure, sought mostly to empower and enrich himself and the Liberal Party. But even with all the bumbling, duplicity, and abuse of power that was the hallmark of the Chretien Liberals for a decade, the biggest scandal to hit his government had yet to be made public.

CHAPTER EIGHT

YOUR MONEY, THEIR FRIENDS

O n February 10, 2004 Auditor General Sheila Fraser released her "Government-Wide Audit of Sponsorship, Advertising and Public Opinion Research" which found the federal government under Chretien "ran the Sponsorship program in a way that showed little regard for Parliament" with "widespread non-compliance with contracting rules" under federal law.[278] The *Toronto Star* headline the next day captured the essence of how the Chretien Liberals viewed the Sponsorship program:"Your money, their friends."[279]

The *Star* headline came after Fraser found "outrageous" and perhaps even criminal misuse of taxpayers' money to the tune of at least $100 million. This was money that was paid to advertising firms – mainly in Quebec – that had ties to the federal Liberals. The firms were supposed to serve as middlemen in the purchase of $150 million in advertising and sponsorship. Fraser said in a news conference,"This is just such a blatant misuse of public funds. It is shocking."[280] The allegations were serious enough that the RCMP was called upon to conduct 13 investigations into the sponsorship scandal.

The fallout of the news of the scandal, which *National Post* columnist Andrew Coyne called Adscam[281], prompted the new Prime Minister, Paul Martin, to recall former Minister of Public Works Alphonso Gagliano from his relatively new post as the ambassador to Denmark. The scandal would subsequently result in several more dismissals of bureaucrats with long-standing ties to the Chretien government: Gagliano's former chief of staff Pierre Tremblay was removed from his post at the Canadian Food Inspection Agency, former Chretien chief of staff Jean Pelletier was dismissed as chairman of VIA Rail, and former Foreign Affairs Minister Andre Oullette was ousted as the head of Canada Post. Chretien's patronage may have rewarded his able lieutenants for their loyalty but it would not protect them from taking responsibility for their role in the abuse of taxpayers' dollars in the sponsorship scandal.

While it was Martin who was left to deal with Adscam and its political consequences, this particular case is the emblematic scandal of Chretien's decade in power. With four out of every ten Sponsorship Program dollars going for commissions to companies with ties to the Liberal Party, it became clear that the program was little more than a slush fund for the party in Quebec. What excuse would Chretien have for the so-called systemic irregularities that persisted for six years at Public Works and the Sponsorship Program? The specifics of the Auditor General's Report and the bluntness of Sheila Fraser's condemnation of the government's actions and attitudes were startling, beginning with the opening sentence: "From 1997 until 31 August 2001, the federal government ran the Sponsorship Program in a way that showed little regard for Parliament, the *Financial Administration Act*, contracting rules and regulations, transparency, and value for money."[282]

Fraser found that "those responsible for the program broke the government's own rules in the way they selected communications agencies and awarded contracts to them," that "some sponsorship funds were transferred to Crown corporations using unusual methods that appear designed to provide significant commissions to communications agencies, while hiding the source of funds and the true nature of the transactions," that "documentation was very poor" and that there "was little evidence of analysis to support the expenditure of $250 million."[283]

Furthermore, the Auditor General found "communications agencies were paid significant sums by CCSB to simply deliver cheques to the corporations," many in violation of at least one aspect of "the Government Contracts Regulations, the *Financial Administration Act*, financial and contracting policies of Crown corporations," and the Treasury Board's own rules on payments and transfers.[284]

It doesn't take an auditor to understand that rules were broken when "a number of transactions" used "false invoices and contracts or no written communications at all." But why would this occur? The AG Report suggests, "these arrangements appear designed to provide commissions to communications agencies, while hiding the source of funds and the true nature of the transactions."[285] The *Ottawa Citizen* reported that Gagliano bragged that he "work[ed] with few tools: no pens, no paper."[286] The paper said, "there exists virtually no paper trail to back up what could have been mistaken for a political money-laundering scheme for the Liberals." Liberal partisans say that is proof that no such scheme existed; skeptics say it is proof that the Chretien Liberals were clever.

Norman Steinberg, head of the audit and ethics branch of the Public Works Department, confirmed Fraser's findings that rules were routinely skirted. When he testified before the Parliamentary Public Accounts committee in March 2004, Steinberg said the department "broke every rule in the book."

Created in the wake of the October 1995 referendum in which Canada could have been broken apart by a separatist vote in Quebec, the Sponsorship Program was to provide money to cultural and community organizations and events in exchange for federal "visibility," defined as displaying Canadian symbols such as the Canada wordmark, maple leaf, Canadian flag, or other explicitly federalist logos. From 1997 until August of 2001, the government paid $250 million to sponsor 1,987 events (the "vast majority" in Quebec[287]), with nearly 40 per cent of the money going to communications agencies as production fees and commissions.

The Auditor General found that there had been oddities from the very inception of the program: the federal government "did not inform Parliament of the programs' real objectives" nor "has it ever reported its results." While a former official with the Communications Co-ordination Services Branch (CCSB) of Public Works told the Auditor General that the government wanted to raise "its profile in Quebec" the AG "saw no such direction from government and no formal analysis or strategic plan."[288] The Auditor General found that Public Works and Government Services Canada, a Department of Public Works which oversaw the CCSB (which itself oversaw the federal communications initiatives including the Sponsorship Program), never even mentioned the Sponsorship Program in its reports until 2001.

Why would this happen? How could it happen? Why the secrecy?

The answers are probably all connected: Chretien. The Chretien government sought to raise the profile of the country in Quebec to help prevent another close separatist vote and assist Liberal-friendly firms at the same time. What order of importance these two goals had for Chretien and his PMO is a matter only they can answer.

The most charitable reading is that like a mob boss or local thug, Chretien instinctively paid off his Liberal cronies; it was second nature to him to help his friends and allies even when doing the right thing. How they allowed this to happen was outlined by Fraser's report: "The Sponsorship Program operated in a weak control environment," with little financial oversight and decisions about communications agencies chosen and events to be sponsored made by "only a few individuals." Oddly the "same individuals who approved the projects also approved invoices for payment" and thus "roles and responsibilities were not segregated to eliminate, as far as possible, any opportunities for fraud and misstatement or an override of controls by management."[289]

When Ranald Quail, a former deputy minister in the Public Works Department under Alphonso Gagliano, testified before the House of Commons Public Accounts Committee on March 1, 2004, he said that everything about the Sponsorship Program was done differently than the other programs at Public Works. Normally, Quail oversaw all negotiations and deals between bureaucrats and the cabinet minister in charge of Public Works. However, he said that Gagliano, Chretien's Quebec lieutenant, approved an unorthodox management structure. The usual operation was for the government to handle spending in two steps, with two different people involved. The first person would sign a contract with a company, and the second person ensured the product or service was delivered before payment was approved. Quail testified that Gagliano "wanted CCSB to be the group responsible in totality for sponsorships."

Committee member and Liberal MP Joe Jordan recognized the problem with the management structure. Jordan says combining the decision-making process with the approval of invoices "violates one-over-one approval." He said that the CCSB was effectively a rogue part of government, spending "money as if it were its own."

But according to Quail, the pressure to run the program this way may have come from the highest tiers of the Ottawa power structure. He said there was political interference from the highest echelons of power in the decision-making process in terms of which events would be funded and which firms would get the contracts. Indeed, this may be the most serious allegation in the Sponsorship scandal, but one that has received relatively little attention.

Quail testified that there was a "very direct relationship" between senior political officials, including those in the PMO, and Chuck Guite, the top bureaucrat in charge of the Sponsorship Program. He also claimed that Chretien personally signed off on a request to the Treasury Board for increased CCSB funding.

When Quail returned May 5 to testify before the Public Accounts committee, he was more specific in describing the nature of the political involvement. He said the Privy Council Office was "part of signing of the Treasury Board submissions. In order to get a signature on a submission, you had to have a discussion with somebody in the PCO who works in (the Prime Minister's Office) to go to the prime minister and get it signed. So, in actual fact, we did have discussions." Gagliano, Guite and Pelletier would meet to discuss the "selection lists" and determine which events would get sponsorship money. The *Toronto Star* summarized Quail's testimony: "It was abnormal for a middle-level public works official like Guite to go around his deputy minister to talk regularly with the Public Works minister and the prime minister's chief of staff."[290]

Isabelle Roy, a former top aide to Gagliano, also testified that there was high-level political input, saying that Gagliano himself was involved in the decision-making process. On April 20, she told the Public Accounts committee that the minister "strongly recommended" certain applications for sponsorship money be approved. She would meet Guite at least once a month on behalf of the minister to discuss specific applications.

She also said the PMO and Chretien's riding office were regularly involved in putting "pressure" on top officials for specific sponsorship grants and that Chretien chief-of-staff Jean Pelletier met with Guite regularly to discuss the Sponsorship Program. Furthermore, Denis Coderre, a former minister of amateur sport and the president of the powerful and influential Privy Council, also contacted the Public Works Department regarding the Sponsorship Program. She alleged that Coderre couldn't get the Treasury Board or the Finance Department to fund specific amateur sporting events in Quebec, so he relied on the Sponsorship Program to funnel money to those events instead.

Roy, who was a liaison between the minister's office and the CCSB when she worked directly for Gagliano, also testified that her duties were expanded in 1999 when she joined the communications branch to include reviewing all sponsorship applications and to make recommendations on which projects to fund. She said the "minister's office had a strong interest in how the program was managed" but that almost all communication between the Sponsorship Program and Gagliano's office were verbal – that is, without any documentation or paper trail.

Reverting to form, Chretien himself would defend the Sponsorship Program and excuse the misuse of funds while preparing for a speech in London, England in March 2004. He said that the program was defensible considering Canada as we know it almost came to end in the '95 referendum: "It was a very useful program to sell Canada to people who wanted to separate from Canada." However, Sheila Fraser found no evidence that the sponsorships were effective or even that there was increased federal visibility in Quebec as a result of the expenditures.

Whether or not the program was designed with laudable goals, and regardless of its efficacy, there remained the issue of the $100 million that went to firms with ties to the Liberal Party, and the spending that remained unaccounted for. Chretien insisted that any problems with the program were administrative. The (by-now-former) Prime Minister admitted he knew there were problems when he was still in office "That's nothing new. It's a problem of accounting."

Testifying before the Public Works committee, Pelletier admitted he met Guite but denied that it amounted to political interference. He also defended the abuse of taxpayers' money, saying the government was fighting to keep Quebec part of the country; implying that $100 million was a reasonable price to pay to keep the country together. But few critics were questioning the sponsorship program itself; rather, the Auditor-General, the Opposition and the media wondered why it was necessary to spend such proportionately large amounts – basically a 66 percent commission – on $150 million in sponsorships.

The program seemed designed to allow minimum oversight and was thus vulnerable to political interference. The Auditor General's Report found that from 1997 until April 1, 2000, "the Sponsorship Program operated with no guidelines." Thus, personal and possibly political decisions could be made about what events to sponsor and how much to pay communications firms handling the account. Public Affairs Committee chair John Williams said the lobbying by senior members of the government, especially the PMO, indicated that the Sponsorship Program was "a politically motivated program where the rules didn't apply and politics was the overriding agenda." The Auditor General's Report "found it impossible in most cases to determine why an event was selected for sponsorship, how the dollar value of a sponsorship was determined, or what federal visibility the sponsorship would achieve."[291] Perhaps only Chretien's staff knew.

Fraser castigated the government for using "highly complicated and questionable methods to transfer sponsorship funds" with "some payments [to Crown corporations] based on artificial invoices and contracts" while some sponsorship to Crown corporations were little more than "subsidies – sponsorship money used by the Crown corporations to cover their normal operating costs."[292] What made such sponsorships especially odd was that since 1998, Crown corporations had been required by law to display a Canada wordmark or similar logo. The Auditor General found no "evidence of additional visibility purchased with the sponsorship fund."[293]

The aspect of this scandal, nicely encapsulated by the headline, that has made it stick is the easy-to-understand funneling of money to firms with ties to the Liberal Party; more than any other scandal, the abuse of the public purse for the benefit of the Liberal Party and its friends that is at the center of Adscam was as simple as it was abhorrent.

Many of the commissions went to Groupaction Marketing, a Quebec advertising firm with connections to the Liberal Party. On April 7, Alain Richard, the former vice-president of Groupaction, said his firm had an "IOU relationship" with Liberal politicians. He told the House of Commons Public Accounts committee that Groupaction did work for the Liberals in the federal election "at very advantageous rates" and in return "when the party is in power, they remit contracts from such Crown corporations as Canada Post, VIA Rail and Tourism Canada."[294] It appeared that the Liberal government of Jean Chretien considered the Sponsorship Program a giant slush fund for its Quebec allies. Groupaction also made a $70,000 donation to the federal Liberals.

A preliminary 2002 audit found that Groupaction was paid $1.6 million for a pro-federalism advertising campaign and a series of reports. That audit found that the awarding of the contracts to Groupaction broke "every rule in the book"; afterward, the RCMP investigated the Montreal-based firm. The audit also revealed that the company never provided all the services the government had paid for, including a $540,990 report that was never found and that on another occasion it filed a report almost identical to one it had previously submitted. Of course, each report was paid for separately.

It is especially disturbing to consider that Sheila Fraser found the Sponsorship Program paid commissions in a manner seemingly designed to hide the nature of the transaction. This would suggest that the government knew that the money paid to these firms was, at the very least, suspect and that the suspicions these transactions might raise would invite unwelcome scrutiny of the entire program.

In February, Richard told the *Globe and Mail* that his company made hundreds of false claims, charging the government for hours that were never worked and bilking taxpayers out of millions of dollars.

Le Groupe Polgone Editeurs Inc., another Quebec firm with Liberal connections, also won lucrative contracts from Ottawa after the Quebec referendum. The firm, of which Liberal cabinet minister Denis Coderre was once vice-president of public affairs and whose consultant Jacques Corriveau was a personal friend of Chretien's, received almost $40 million in government sponsorship funds. Among the commissions was a payment for $330,000 for a hunting and fishing show which had been scheduled for the year 2000. The show never happened.

The gravity of the scandal was further driven home on May 10, 2004 when two central figures in the controversy were arrested by the RCMP: Charles Guite, the senior bureaucrat, and Jean Brault, president of Groupaction Marketing. The two men were charged with five counts of fraud and one count of conspiracy to commit fraud relating to contracts awarding the communications firm from 1996-1999.

It is not just that often-exorbitant commissions were paid to Liberal-friendly firms; the way in which the firms were selected also raised eyebrows. Fraser's report says that "the selection process [of communications agencies] did not comply with the Government Contracts Regulations" and that there was no evidence "that the specific requirements of the work were ever advertised or documented."[295] A majority of the files audited "contained no assessment of the project's merits or even any criteria for assessing merit" or even "the rationale for supporting the decision to sponsor" the specific event.[296] Furthermore, there was little or no analysis that the government had received what it was paying for or whether it got value for sponsorship.[297]

While Chretien claimed to be interested in using sponsorship of community events as a way of fostering pro-federalist sentiment in Quebec, he did not seem to have much interest in ascertaining whether the program worked. According to Chretien, administrative errors and obscenely large commissions were a small price to pay for national unity. More importantly, his dismissal of the entire scandal as nothing but a series of "administrative" errors reflected an arrogant nonchalance about procedure. It's almost as if he considered himself and his staff to be beyond rules, regulations, procedures, and processes. The Auditor General found that the Sponsorship Program "bypassed" the "Parliamentary process."[298] Once again, Chretien, his cabinet ministers and the PMO operated with little regard for the role of Parliament or the formalities of democratic rule. It seems that in their arrogance, they viewed those formalities as mere "technicalities" that could be ignored at will.

The Natural Governing Party had transformed governance in Ottawa into a One-Party State. And within that One-Party State, the actual power to govern and make decisions was concentrated in the hands of a small cadre of Chretien loyalists. Perhaps Chretien was right; maybe the Sponsorship Program *was* a worthwhile and necessary endeavour to keep Quebec in confederation. But even if that were the case, the government was obliged to go to Parliament to justify the expenditure of a quarter of a billion dollars on this endeavour. But that never happened. After a decade in power, the Chretien cadre apparently no longer saw any need to discuss or obtain approval for any policy or expenditure. The arrogance had reached its apex. The wishes of the anointed few would suffice.

SO... WHAT NOW?

during Jean Chretien's time in office, there were major changes in Ottawa. Chretien changed the function of the Prime Minister's office, continuing a trend that had begun under his mentor, Pierre Trudeau. He greatly centralized power and decision-making to the detriment of democracy. But Chretien also transformed the way Canadians view the "office" of Prime Minister – the very function and purpose of the position. In some sense, Canadians are fortunate that Chretien had no greater ambition than to attain and hold power for its own sake, and perhaps reward a few friends in the process. If he had truly been an ideologue with evil designs to radically transform the country, he had accrued enough power to himself and his office that he would likely have gotten away with it.

The decade-long rule of Jean Chretien is a real-life Aesop's fable, a lesson for democracies of what can happen when a country has an inattentive public, a negligent media and an ineffective Opposition. There will always be corrupt and arrogant leaders, but their potential to inflict harm on the country is usually attenuated when others – citizens, journalists and opposition politicians – fulfill their responsibilities.

So what now for Canada? The political landscape was beginning to change in the months before the Adscam scandal broke open. The NDP had, for the first time since the 1980s, a dynamic, determined and intelligent leader in Jack Layton – a man who was fearless and smart in his attacks on the Liberals from the Left. As Layton often said, it would behoove the Liberals well to look over their left shoulder. The Conservatives were united again after the Tories and Canadian Alliance voted in December 2003 to merge their parties. Stephen Harper, a smart, unthreatening conservative populist able to reach beyond a narrow scope of the political spectrum, leads the new Conservative Party. With Adscam as the latest, easiest-to-understand scandal – as encapsulated in that four-word headline in the *Star* – the Liberals looked beatable for the first time since before Chretien became leader. It is a curious but delicious irony that the 11-year reign of the Natural Governing Party looked ready to come to a premature end just as the popular former finance minister – a man who had been grooming himself for the position for most of his life – was ready to take the helm.

With the prospect of losing his majority, to say nothing of not making the expected gains that many pundits were predicting when Martin assumed the office of Prime Minister, Martin was forced to hold a quick election as he had promised. Speculation of an April election soon gave way to a May election, then an early June campaign, before finally being called for June 28. It was repeatedly postponed so Parliament could investigate the Adscam scandal. Despite promising not to hold an election until all the facts of the sponsorship scandal were made public, Martin closed Parliament early, obstructing the investigation of the Public Accounts committee in the process. Was Martin going to follow Chretien's lead and obstruct an investigation into the Liberal government's wrong-doings? More importantly, would voters be as forgiving of the Liberal government's series of scandals in 2004 as it had been in 2000?

There is a story about a historian who was asked at the beginning of the 20th century whether the French Revolution had succeeded. He replied that it was too early to tell. It will not be clear until at least the next election (if not later) what the 2004 federal election portends for Canada's political future. With Paul Martin's Liberals reduced to a minority (135 seats) and the Conservatives growing to 99, there may well be a significant political shift beginning, a reconsideration of the Liberal birthright to govern Canada and of Liberal values being synonymous with Canadian values.

But there are two other possibilities, neither of which is as encouraging. The first possibility is that reducing the Liberals to a minority government is the voters' way of punishing the Liberal Party; a signal that the government can't do anything it wants with perpetual immunity and a warning that if they continue to try, they could (theoretically) be removed from office. The second possibility is that Canada is becoming more politically polarized with Atlantic and Central Canada supporting the Liberal Party and the West and parts of rural Ontario voting Conservative.[xv.]

Sadly only a large-scale political realignment, including a demonstrated willingness on the part of Canadian voters to consider voting non-Liberal would be likely to change the Liberal party's ways; that realignment would have to include the very real and demonstrable possibility that the party might lose power altogether. If Paul Martin does not see his minority government as a wake-up call from voters,

---

xv. A third "polarization" – if you will excuse the impossibility of being polarized among three points – is the Bloc Quebecois in la belle province. The Bloc vote seems to be an anti-Liberal government vote, or perhaps just a vote against the government of the day. The practical consequence of the Bloc's majority status in Quebec is that it will make forming a majority government in Ottawa, especially for the Conservatives, more difficult.

the lesson of the 2004 election could easily be lost on the Liberals. Or they might even construe it as an endorsement to continue with business as usual.

Ultimately, the antidote to Liberal arrogance lies in the power of voters to throw the party out of office. That power, should it be exercised, would be a useful reminder that it is not the birthright of the Liberal Party to rule Canada. But ultimately it will be up to Canadians if they want to continue to live in a One-Party State run by, of and for the few.

ENDNOTES

1. Michael Bliss, *Right Honourable Men: Revised and Updated* (Toronto: HarperCollins, 2004) p. 313.
2. Jean Chretien, quoted in Edison Stewart, "Liberal free vote plan would give MPs greater clout," *Toronto Star*, January 20, 1993.
3. David Frum, "Breaking through Liberal mind control," *Western Standard*, March 12, 2004.
4. On July 17th, 2003 Cauchon released the government's proposed new bill to legalize gay unions. During that press conference, Cauchon made the statement that same-sex marriage was now a "Canadian value".
5. Susan Delacourt, Les Whittington and Tonda MacCharles, "Your money, their friends," *Toronto Star*, February 11, 2004.
6. J.L. Granatstein, *Who Killed the Canadian Military?* (Toronto: HarperFlamingo Canada, 2004) p. 164.
7. *Ibid*, p. 165.
8. *Ibid*.
9. *Bliss*, p. 323.
10. *Ibid*, p. 323.
11. Jeffrey Simpson, *The Friendly Dictatorship* (Toronto: McClelland & Stewart, 2001) p.188-189.
12. Edward Greenspon and Anthony Wilson-Smith, *Double Vision: The Inside Story of the Liberals in Power* (Toronto: Seal Books, 1998), p. 8-9.
13. Quoted in Greenspon and Wilson-Smith, p. 373.

14. Lawrence Martin, *Iron Man: The Defiant Reign of Jean Chretien* (Toronto: Viking, 2003) p. 154-155.

15. Greenspon and Wilson-Smith, p. 375.

16. Jeffrey Simpson, "And some have honour thrust upon them," *Globe and Mail*, May 2, 1996

17. Jeffrey Simpson, "The promise to scrap the GST had political value but little honesty," *Globe and Mail*, April 23, 1996.

18. Terence Corcoran, "How the Liberals can kill the GST," *Globe and Mail*, May 1, 1996.

19. Greenspon and Wilson-Smith, p. 377.

20. *Ibid*, p. 379-380.

21. Jeffrey Simpson, "And some have honour thrust upon them."

22. *Bliss*, p. 329

23. Jeffrey Simpson, *The Friendly Dictatorship*, p. 41.

24. *Ibid*, p. 80-81.

25. *Ibid*, p. 94.

26. *Ibid*, p.95.

27. Ethel Blondin-Andrews quoted in "No such word as 'scandal'," October 26, 1998, *Western Report*, p. 6.

28. Howard Wilson quoted in "No such word as 'scandal'."

29. David Vienneau, "78% of pledges kept: PM," *Toronto Star*, October 25, 1996.

30. Clyde Graham, "'Acts of God' can kill promises: Chretien," Canadian Press, published in the *London Free Press*, May 3, 1996.

31. Neil Nevitte, Andre Blais, Elisabeth Gidengil and Richard Nadeau, *Unsteady State: The 1997 Canadian Federal Election* (Don Mills: Oxford University Press, 2000) p. 75.

32. "Chretien plans Quebec strategy," Canadian Press, *Globe and Mail*, March 28, 1994.

33. Carol Goar, "The risky business of bestowing goodies on Quebec," *Toronto Star*, April 5, 1994.

34. Joan Bryden, "Prime Minister's lack of strategy to fend off separatism irks critics," *London Free Press*, May 2, 1994.

35. Greenspon and Wilson-Smith, p. 172.

36. "To keep Quebec, Chretien must go," John Crispo, *Toronto Sun*, November 12, 1999. Reprinted in Crispo, *Rebel Without a Pause: Memoirs of a Canadian Maverick* (Toronto: Warwick Publishing, 2002) p. 330.

37. Michael Bliss, p. 318.

38. Heward Graftey, *Democracy Challenged: How to End One-Party Rule in Canada* (Montreal, Vehicule Press, 2002) p. 13.

39. Nevitte *et al*, p. 75.

40. Peter Desbarats, *Somalia Cover-Up: A Commissioner's Journal* (Toronto: McClelland & Stewart, 1999) p. 183

41. *Ibid*, p. 186.

42. Preston Manning, *Think Big: My Adventures in Life and Democracy*
    (Toronto: McCelland & Stewart, 2002) p. 115.
43. Hugh Segal, *In Defence of Civility: Reflections of a Recovering Politician*
    (Toronto: Stoddart, 2000) p. 173.
44. David Collenette, quoted in Desbarats, p. 186.
45. Desbarats, p. 190.
46. Rory Leishman, "Chretien must fire Boyle, Collenette,"
    London Free Press, August 20, 1996.
47. Desbarats, p. 183.
48. *Ibid*, p. 194.
49. *Ibid*, p. 198.
50. *Ibid*, p. 199.
51. *Ibid*, p. 208.
52. Martin, p. 160.
53. Desbarats, p. 209, 213, 246.
54. Martin, p. 161.
55. Diane Francis, "It's appalling military tried to hide the truth,"
    London Free Press, November 1, 1997.
56. Manning, p. 112-113.
57. Martin, p. 205.
58. Manning, p. 113-114.
59. Martin, p. 206.
60. Ibid, p. 204.
61. Ibid, p. 149-150.
62. William Kaplan, *Presumed Guilty: Brian Mulroney, the Airbus Affair
    and the Government of Canada* (Toronto: McCelland & Steward, 1998) p. 270.
63. *Ibid*, p. 285.
64. *Ibid*, p. 289.
65. Martin, p. 151.
66. *Ibid*, p. 152.
67. *Ibid*, p. 152.
68. Kaplan, p. 303.
69. *Ibid*, p. 303-304.
70. J.L. Granatstein and Normal Hiller, *Prime Ministers: Ranking Canada's Leaders*
    (Toronto: HarperCollins, 2000) p. 225
71. Andrew Cohen, *While Canada Slept: How We Lost Our Place in the World*
    (Toronto: McClelland & Stewart, 2003) p. 155-156.
72. Quoted in Martin, p. 173.
73. Simpson, *The Friendly Dictatorship*, p. 76.
74. Manning, p. 160.
75. Martin, p. 168.
76. Ibid, p. 168.
77. Hugh Winsor and Jeff Sallot, "Minority numbers jarred Liberals,"
    Globe and Mail, June 4, 1997.

78. John Duffy, *Fights of Our Lives: Elections, Leadership,
    and the Making of Canada*, (Toronto: HarperCollins, 2002) p. 359.
79. Manning, p. 163-166.
80. Neil Nevitte, *et al*, p. 129.
81. *Ibid*, p. 48-51.
82. *Ibid*, p. 50.
83. *Ibid*, p. 16.
84. R. Kenneth Carty, William Cross and Lisa Young, *Rebuilding Canadian
    Party Politics*, (Vancouver: UBC Press, 2000) p. 77.
85. Nevitte, *et al*, p. 66-78.
86. *Ibid*, p. 127.
87. Peter C. Newman, *Defining Moments: Dispatches from
    an Unfinished Revolution*, (Toronto: Viking, 1997) p. 3.
88. Gordon Gibson, "Something to unsettle everyone,"
    Globe and Mail, June 5, 1997.
89. "Split decision," *Toronto Sun*, June 3, 1997.
90. Carty *et al*, p. 82.
91. Robert Sheppard, "A region called Ontario," *Globe and Mail*, June 5, 1997.
92. *Ibid.*
93. *Ibid.*
94. Robert Sheppard, "Hey, it's still a majority," *Globe and Mail*, June 7, 1997.
95. Winsor and Sallot.
96. Newman, p. 3.
97. Quoted in Graham Fraser, "New Parliament won't be run the same old way,"
    Globe and Mail, June 4, 1997.
98. Gibson.
99. Nevitte et al, p. 134.
100. Don Boudria, quoted in Shafer Parker Jr., "Cool summer, hot fall,"
    Western Report, October 5, 1998, p. 6-7.
101. Martin, p. 198.
102. W. Wesley Pue, editor, *Pepper in Our Eyes: The APEC Affair*
    (Vancouver: UBC Press, 2000).
103. Andrew D. Irvine, "Free Speech, Democracy and the Question
    of Political Influence," in Pue, p. 34.
104. Donald J. Sorochan, QC, "The APEC Protest, the Rule of Law,
    and Civilian Oversight of Canada's National Police Force," in Pue, p. 72.
105. Pue, p. viii.
106. Robert Vanderloo, quoted in Pue, p. xiii.
107. Pue, p. xvi.
108. "A dutiful son," *National Post*, August 28, 1999.
109. "PM's former aide denies arranging APEC security,"
    National Post, August 24, 1999.
110. Shirley Heafy, quoted in "Personal Reflections on the Ill-fated First
    APEC Inquiry," Gerald M. Morin, QC, in Pue (editor), p. 163.

111. Gerald M. Morin, QC, "Personal Reflections on the Ill-fated First APEC Inquiry," in Pue, p. 163.
112. Martin, p. 201.
113. Marcel Pepin, quoted in Pue, p. 21.
114. Pue, p, 9.
115. Numerous contributors to Pue's volume come close to calling Chretien's Canada a police state. For example, Margot E. Young complained about the "authoritarian excess within the Canadian state." (p. 41).
116. Pue, p. 12.
117. *Vancouver Province* columnist Jim McNulty, quoted in Pue, p. 141.
118. Pue, p. 3.
119. "Police, politicians, and accountability in the Canadian Democracy," press release by UBC Press, August 3, 2001.
120. "APEC report released," *Ubyssey*, September 4, 2001.
121. David Charbonneau, "Chretien's attitude towards legitimate protest is not acceptable," *Kamloops Daily News*, August 21, 2001.
122. Pue, p. 24.
123. *Ibid*, p. 13-14.
124. Manning, p. 219.
125. *Ibid*.
126. Martin, p. 254-255.
127. Walter Robinson, "HRDC Boondoggle: Five Questions for Minister Stewart," *Canadian Taxpayer's Federation release*, February 16, 2000.
128. Manning, p. 221.
129. 2000 Report of the Auditor General of Canada, "Chapter 11 Human Resources Development Canada – Grants and Contributions."
130. Manning, p. 221.
131. Martin, p. 255.
132. Manning, p. 220. Professor Michael Smart, an economist at the University of Toronto, told a lunch-time seminar at the Fraser Institute March 5, 2004, that there is ample evidence of the government spending the Transitional Jobs Fund in ridings that were closely contested in recent elections.
133. Robinson. Also, Professor Smart made the same point. See previous endnote.
134. Manning 221.
135. Martin, p. 296.
136. Simpson, *The Friendly Dictatorship*, p. 41-42.
137. Manning, p. 220.
138. Denis Desautels quoted in David A. Good, *The Politics of Public Management* (Toronto: University of Toronto Press, 2003), p. 87.
139. Martin, p. 255
140. Brian Tobin, *All in Good Time* (Toronto: HarperCollins, 2002) p. 241.
141. Lawrence Martin, "Rotten in Denmark," *Globe and Mail*, September 13, 2003.
142. Paul Stanway, "Digging the dirt on Shovelgate," *Edmonton Sun*, February 4, 2000.

143. Martin, Iron Man, p. 299.
144. "Dishonourable conduct," *National Post*, June 2, 2001
145. "Conrad Black finally made a life peer," *Daily Telegraph*, September 12, 2001.
146. "Canadian prime minister blocks Black's life peerage,"
     Daily Telegraph, June 19, 1999.
147. Martin, p. 231.
148. *Ibid*, p. 229.
149. *Ibid*.
150. National Post, June 2, 2001
151. "Lord Black," National Post, November 1, 2001
152. *Ibid*.
153. Martin, p. 229.
154. *National Post*, November 1, 2001
155. Mark Steyn, "Good Lord, deliver us," *National Post*, June 24, 1999.
156. Polls indicated that other issues on which the public agreed with
     Canadian Alliance, such as crime and gun control, did not rate as
     important during the campaign.
157. Paul Bunner, "Unleash the dogs of Liberalism," *The Report*,
     November 6, 2000, p. 10.
158. Bliss, p. 329.
159. "Tories must now go forward and join the Alliance,"
     Toronto Sun, November 28, 2000.
160. Bunner, p. 10-13.
161. Stephen Clarkson, "The Liberal Threepeat: The Multi-System Party in
     the Multi-Party System," in Jon H. Pammett and Christopher Dornan, editors,
     The Canadian General Election of 2000 (Toronto: Dundurn, 2001) p. 13.
162. Peter White and Adam Daifallah, *Gritlock: Are the Liberals in Forever?*
     (Toronto: Canadian Political Bookshelf, 2001) p. 91.
163. *Ibid*, p. 26
164. Jean-Pierre Kingsley, quoted in Kevin Michael Grace, "Eclectica,"
     The Report, January 22, 2001.
165. Clarkson, p. 33
166. Paul Bunner, "The Ontario Course," *The Report*, December 18, 2000, p. 11.
167. White and Daifallah, p. 32.
168. Warren Kinsella, *Kicking Ass in Canadian Politics*,
     (Toronto: Random House of Canada, 2001) p. 129.
169. *Ibid*, p. 131.
170. *Ibid*.
171. *Ibid*, p. 135, 136.
172. Paul Wells, "After all that, nothing settled, nothing learned,"
     National Post, November 28, 2000.
173. Kinsella, p. 132.
174. William Christian, quoted in "Nasty, negative and shallow,"
     Hamilton Spectator, November 25, 2000.

175. See Trevor W. Harrison, *Requiem for a Lightweight: Stockwell Day and Image Politics* (Montreal: Black Rose Books, 2002) p. 86-88. Also, White and Daifallah, p. 32.

176. Trevor W. Harrison, a sociologist at the University of Alberta, says in his anti-Day book *Requiem for a Lightweight*, that the CA leader's social conservatism did not play a role in the party's poorer than expected showing. p. 87.

177. Grafftey, p. 181.

178. Albina Guarnieri, quoted in "Liberal scores victory No. 4," *Toronto Sun*, November 28, 2000.

179. *National Post*, March 14, 2000

180. Simpson, *The Friendly Dictatorship*, p. 124-125.

181. White and Daifallah, p. 189-192, 194, 195.

182. *Ibid*, p. 195.

183. *Ibid*, p. 93.

184. *Ibid*, p. 88.

185. Eli Schuster, "Now a word from our Ontario leader, Paul Martin," *The Report*, December 18, 2000, p. 13.

186. David Frum, "Paul Martin mistake could unite the right," January 17, 1998, *London Free Press*.

187. Bliss, p. 320.

188. Stephen Harper quoted in Kevin Michael Grace, "An illusion of action," October 21, 2002, *The Report*.

189. "December 2002 Report," Chapter 10, Section 10.1, Office of the Auditor General.

190. "What did taxpayers get for their billion dollars?" press release, Garry Breitkreuz, November 29, 2002.

191. Auditor General's Report (2002), Section 10.53.

192. "Gun Registry could cost $2 billion, critics warn," *Canadian Press*, reprinted on globeandmail.com, March 24, 2003.

193. Breitkreuz.

194. Peter Stock, "Sinking fast," *The Report*, p. 24-25.

195. David Frum, *The Right Man: The Surprise Presidency of George W. Bush: An Inside Account* (New York: Random House, 2003) p. 149-150.

196. Cohen, p. 188.

197. Jason Kenney, quoted on the CBC, November 26, 2002.

198. CBC, November 26, 2002.

199. Bliss, p. 325.

200. Robert Fulford, "US bashing is no longer a game," *National Post*, September 14, 2001.

201. Jean Chretien quoted in Maria McClintock, "Chretien: We're best. Touts Canadian virtues over US," *Toronto Sun*, May 15, 2003.

202. Martin, p. 90.

203 "PM's power threatens to even make cabinet irrelevant," Elizabeth Thompson, *Ottawa Citizen,* reprinted in the *Montreal Gazette,* September 30, 2002.

204. Janko Peric quoted in Steven Chase, "Liberal MPs want details on Kyoto," October 9, 2002, *Globe and Mail.*

205. Tony Valeri quoted in Chase.

206. David Bercuson and Barry Cooper, "PM wants us to believe he is saving the planet," *Calgary Herald,* November 20, 2002

207. Ezra Levant, *Fight Kyoto: The Plan to Protect Our Economic Future* (Calgary: JMCK Publishing, 2002) p. 180.

208. Bercuson and Cooper.

209. Levant, p. 221.

210. Rory Leishman, "At the very least, judges should consult Parliament when they decide to change laws," *The Report,* June 11, 2001.

211. Martin, p. 422.

212. Stephen Harper quoted in "An illusion of action," Kevin Michael Grace, October 21, 2002, *The Report,* p. 16.

213. Susan Delacourt, *Juggernaut: Paul Martin's Campaign for Chretien's Crown* (Toronto: McClelland & Stewart, 2003) p. 103-104.

214. *Ibid,* p. 122.

215. Martin, p. 259-261. Delacourt tells essentially the same story, p. 144-146.

216. Delacourt, p. 218.

217. John Gray, *Paul Martin: The Power of Ambition* (Toronto: Key Porter, 2003), p.104-105. p.180-181.

218. Delacourt, p. 139-141. Martin, p. 241.

219. Martin, p. 243

220. Delacourt, p. 155-162.

221. *Ibid,* p. 157.

222. Martin, p. 271.

223. *Ibid,* p. 271-272.

224. Delacourt, p. 162, Lawrence Martin reports that Aline Chretien said "They're not going to push you out." p. 272.

225. For the record, Brian Tobin says that "the broadband issue did not make me decide to leave politics," although it did "nudge" him to examine his life, an examination that led him to leave politics. Tobin, *All in Good Time,* p. 252.

226. Delacourt, p. 221.

227. Simpson, p. 12.

228. Tobin, p. 247.

229. Clarkson, p. 32.

230. Tobin, p. 247.

231. Simpson, p. 9-10.

232. Delacourt, p. 209.

233. Eddie Goldenberg, quoted in Martin, p. 371.

234. Delacourt, p. 261. Tobin, p. 241.

235. Gray, p.173.

236. "PM's power threatens to even make cabinet irrelevant," Elizabeth Thompson, *Ottawa Citizen*, reprinted in the *Montreal Gazette*, September 30, 2002.

237. Patrick Boyer, quoted in Kevin Michael Grace, "Parliament of ombudsmen," *The Report*, June 11, 2001.

238. Delacourt, p. 146-147.

239. Bliss, p. 330.

240. Donald J. Savoie, *Governing from the Centre: The Concentration of Power in Canadian Politics* (Toronto: University of Toronto Press, 1999) p. 171.

241. Thompson.

242. Thompson.

243. Gordon Robertson, quoted in Thompson.

244. Savoie, p. 97.

245. Simpson, p. 35.

246. *Ibid*, p. 14.

247. *Ibid*, p. 174.

248. Ralph Goodale, quoted in Wilson-Smith and Greenspon, p. 211.

249. Savoie, quoted in Thompson.

250. White and Daifallah, p. 49.

251. Nevitte, et al, p. 61.

252. White and Daifallah, p. 88.

253. *Ibid*.

254. *Ibid*, p. 87.

255. *Ibid*.

256. Neil Nevitte et al, p. 58, 64.

257. *Ibid*, p. 64.

258. Simpson, p. 138.

259. See, for example, Maude Barlow and Bruce Campbell, *Straight Through the Heart* (Toronto: HarperCollins, 1995)

260. Will Ferguson, *Bastards and Boneheads* (Vancouver: Douglas & McIntyre, 1999) p.287.

261. Andrew Coyne, "Why it matters," *National Post*, April 6, 2001.

262 Denyse O'Leary on *Behind the Story*, CTS, February 15, 2004.

263. Simpson, p. 79.

264. J.L. Granatstein and Normal Hiller called the first Liberal term "warmed-over Mulroney." In *Prime Ministers: Ranking Canada's Leaders*, p. 227.

265. *Ibid*.

266. There is, of course, disagreement. Maude Barlow in *Straight Through the Heart* complained of Chretien being Mulroney lite, accepting free trade and balanced budgets; the NDP maintained (and still do) that there is little difference between a Liberal and Conservative. Despite David Frum's aforementioned observation that conservatives had little to complain about the Chretien government, most conservatives thought Chretien did not cut taxes, government spending or the debt far or fast enough.

267. Newman, p. 172.

268. *Ibid*, p. 173.

269. Martin, p. 427.

270. Ted Byfield, "Welcome to Chretien Canada, where sleaze and rot are resoundingly returned to office," *The Report*, December 18, 2000, p. 60.

271. Link Byfield, "Ontarians may be slow learners, but perhaps it's too soon to give up hope," *Western Report*, June 16, 1997.

272. Grafftey, p. 122.

273. Ted Byfield.

274. Tobin, p. 259-260.

275. Interview with Stephen LeDrew, "Covering the Liberal Waterfront: Reflections on a One-Party State," *Policy Options*, March 2003, p. 5-6.

276. Newman, p. 172.

277. Office of the Auditor General, "Government-Wide Audit of Sponsorship, Advertising and Public Opinion Research," November 2003, Sections 1 and 4.

278. Susan Delacourt, Les Whittington and Tonda MacCharles, "Your money, their friends," *Toronto Star*, February 11, 2004.

279. Sheila Fraser quoted in Delacourt *et al*.

280. Andrew Coyne on his weblog www.andrewcoyne.com

281. Office of the Auditor General, Section 3.1.

282. *Ibid.*

283. *Ibid*, Section 3.43.

284. *Ibid* Section 3.44.

285. Jack Aubry, "Gagliano's habits were his undoing," February 11, 2004, *Ottawa Citizen*.

286. Office of the Auditor General, Section 3.17.

287. *Ibid*, Section 3.14.

288. *Ibid*, Section 3.22.

289. "Sponsorship funds allocation 'political' operation, MPs told," May 6, 2004, *Toronto Star*.

290. Office of the Auditor General, Section 3.23.

291. *Ibid*, Section 3.36.

292. *Ibid*, Section 3.40.

293. Alain Richard quoted in Jack Aubry, "Free election work led to sponsorship contracts," April 8, 2004, *Ottawa Citizen*.

294. Office of the Auditor General, Section 3.51.

295. *Ibid*, Section 3.60.

296. *Ibid*, Sections 3.69-3.73, 3.86.

297. *Ibid*, Sections 3.100-3.102.

INDEX

ABOUT THE AUTHOR

Paul Tuns is a public affairs commentator and political analyst whose articles have appeared in more than 35 publications including *the National Post, Globe and Mail* and *Toronto Star*. He is the editor-in-chief of *The Interim*, Canada's life and family newspaper, and a contributor to *Business Report*. He is also a regular panelist on CTS's *Behind The Story,* and a frequent contributor to the book section of *the Halifax Herald*. He lives in Toronto with his wife and three children.

ABOUT FREEDOM PRESS (CANADA) INC

Freedom Press (Canada) Inc. is an independant book publisher dedicated to publishing excellent books that promote a social conservative view of culture, society, civil government and social action.

OTHER BOOKS BY *FREEDOM PRESS*

Rev. Tristan Emmanuel's new book *Christophobia: The Real Reason Behind Hate Crimes Legislation.*

This book is about Bill C-250. Before it died with the adjournment of Canada's Parliament on Nov. 12, 2003, Bill C-250 was known as "an Act to amend the Criminal Code of Canada (hate propaganda)."Actually, to be more precise, this book is about legal oppression. Bill C-250, or whatever the Government of Canada may choose to replace it with in the future, represented the latest legislative initiative to silence moral disapproval of homosexuality. And ultimately, Bill C-250 represented an attempt to suppress the Christian Gospel. The Bill was the legal face of a very real problem: Christophobia.

WHAT OTHERS ARE SAYING:

"Complacent Christian Beware. If you thought the gay rights movement was just about 'tolerance', and that 'discrimination' is anti-scriptural and immoral, think again. This deft, compact book examines the lethal threat to religious liberty posed by the rising demand for special 'hate laws' to protect homosexuals. Emmanuel explores the terrible paradox wherein gays, who no longer suffer any measurable discrimination at all, angrily seek to suppress the most basic rights of Christians, who on all sides are openly defamed, deplored, mocked and marginalized. Clearly, calmly and boldly, he explains why Christians must stop apologizing, stop hiding, and stop pretending they can coexist peacefully with the perverse new faith that has seized control of North American culture." *Link Byfield, Citizen's Centre for Freedom and Democracy, Former publisher of the Alberta Report*

www.freedompress.ca

Printed in the United States
33695LVS00004B/217-237

9 780973 275728